TRANSPORTATION ISSUES, POLICIES AND R&D

AIRLINE PILOTS AND AVIATION PROFESSIONALS

SUPPLY AND DEMAND ISSUES

TRANSPORTATION ISSUES, POLICIES AND R&D

Additional books in this series can be found on Nova's website under the Series tab.

Additional e-books in this series can be found on Nova's website under the e-book tab.

TRANSPORTATION ISSUES, POLICIES AND R&D

AIRLINE PILOTS AND AVIATION PROFESSIONALS

SUPPLY AND DEMAND ISSUES

ANGELA DILLINGER
EDITOR

publishers

New York

Library of Congress Cataloging-in-Publication Data

ISBN: 978-1-63321-035-6

Published by Nova Science Publishers, Inc. † New York

CONTENTS

PREFACE

This book describes what available data and forecasts reveal about the need for and potential availability of airline pilots, and what actions industry and government are taking or could take to attract and retain airline pilots. It then discusses what available data and forecasts reveal about the need for and potential availability of aerospace engineers, aircraft mechanics, and avionics technicians, and what actions industry and the federal government are taking to help attract and retain these professionals.

Chapter 1 – Over 66,000 airline pilot jobs exist for larger mainline and smaller regional airlines that operate over 7,000 commercial aircraft. After a decade of turmoil that curtailed growth in the industry and resulted in fewer pilots employed at airlines since 2000, recent industry forecasts indicate that the global aviation industry is poised for growth. However, stakeholders have voiced concerns that imminent retirements, fewer pilots exiting the military, and new rules increasing the number of flight hours required to become a first officer for an airline, could result in a shortage of qualified airline pilots.

GAO was asked to examine pilot supply and demand issues. This report describes (1) what available data and forecasts reveal about the need for and potential availability of airline pilots and (2) what actions industry and government are taking or could take to attract and retain airline pilots. GAO collected and analyzed data from 2000 through 2012, forecasts from 2013 through 2022, and literature relevant to the labor market for airline pilots and reviewed documents and interviewed agency officials about programs that support training. GAO interviewed and collected data from associations representing airlines or their pilots, and pilot schools that accounted for about half of the students who graduated with professional pilot majors in 2012. GAO selected the airlines and schools based on factors such as size and location. GAO is not making recommendations in this report. The Department of Transportation and others provided technical clarifications on a draft of the report, which GAO incorporated.

Chapter 2 – Maintaining a safe and robust aviation system requires qualified aviation professionals—including aerospace engineers, aircraft mechanics, and avionics technicians—to design, manufacture, and repair more than 225,000 aircraft. Aviation stakeholders have expressed concerns that an insufficient supply of personnel could develop because of imminent retirements and a perception that fewer people enter these professions.

GAO was asked to review the supply and demand of aviation professionals. This report discusses (1) what available data and forecasts reveal about the need for and potential availability of aerospace engineers, aircraft mechanics, and avionics technicians, and (2) what actions industry and the federal government are taking to help attract and retain these professionals. GAO (1) collected and analyzed data from 2000 through 2012, employment projections from 2012 through 2022, and literature relevant to the aviation professionals' labor markets; (2) reviewed agency documents; and (3) interviewed agency officials about programs that support training. GAO also interviewed 10 aviation industry associations (5 representing employees and 5 representing employers) and selected a non-generalizable sample of 23 private sector employers, based on size and location, to understand any actions used to attract their workforce.

GAO is not making recommendations. GAO received technical comments on this report from Education, DOL, and DOT, which were incorporated as appropriate. DOD did not have any comments on this report.

In: Airline Pilots and Aviation Professionals   ISBN: 978-1-63321-035-6
Editor: Angela Dillinger   © 2014 Nova Science Publishers, Inc.

Chapter 1

AVIATION WORKFORCE: CURRENT AND FUTURE AVAILABILITY OF AIRLINE PILOTS[*]

United States Government Accountability Office

WHY GAO DID THIS STUDY

Over 66,000 airline pilot jobs exist for larger mainline and smaller regional airlines that operate over 7,000 commercial aircraft. After a decade of turmoil that curtailed growth in the industry and resulted in fewer pilots employed at airlines since 2000, recent industry forecasts indicate that the global aviation industry is poised for growth. However, stakeholders have voiced concerns that imminent retirements, fewer pilots exiting the military, and new rules increasing the number of flight hours required to become a first officer for an airline, could result in a shortage of qualified airline pilots.

GAO was asked to examine pilot supply and demand issues. This report describes (1) what available data and forecasts reveal about the need for and potential availability of airline pilots and (2) what actions industry and government are taking or could take to attract and retain airline pilots. GAO collected and analyzed data from 2000 through 2012, forecasts from 2013 through 2022, and literature relevant to the labor market for airline pilots and reviewed documents and interviewed agency officials about programs that support training. GAO interviewed and collected data from associations

---

[*] This is an edited, reformatted and augmented version of United States Government Accountability Office Publication, No. GAO-14-232, dated February 2014.

representing airlines or their pilots, and pilot schools that accounted for about half of the students who graduated with professional pilot majors in 2012. GAO selected the airlines and schools based on factors such as size and location. GAO is not making recommendations in this report. The Department of Transportation and others provided technical clarifications on a draft of the report, which GAO incorporated.

WHAT GAO FOUND

GAO found mixed evidence regarding the extent of a shortage of airline pilots, although regional airlines have reported difficulties finding sufficient numbers of qualified pilots over the past year. Specifically, looking at broad economic indicators, airline pilots have experienced a low unemployment rate—the most direct measure of a labor shortage; however, both employment and earnings have decreased since 2000, suggesting that demand for these occupations has not outstripped supply. Looking forward, industry forecasts and the Bureau of Labor Statistics' employment projections suggest the need for pilots to be between roughly 1,900 and 4,500 pilots per year, on average, over the next decade, which is consistent with airlines' reported expectations for hiring over this period. Yet studies GAO reviewed examining whether the future supply of pilots will be sufficient to meet this need had varying conclusions. Two studies point to the large number of qualified pilots that exists, but who may be working abroad, in the military, or in another occupation, as evidence that there is adequate supply. However, whether these pilots choose to seek employment with U.S. airlines depends on the extent to which pilot job opportunities arise, and on the wages and benefits airlines offer. Another study concludes that future supply will be insufficient, absent any actions taken, largely resulting from accelerating costs of pilot education and training. Such costs deter individuals from pursuing a pilot career. Pilot schools that GAO interviewed reported fewer students entering their programs resulting from concerns over the high costs of education and low entry-level pay at regional airlines. As airlines have recently started hiring, nearly all of the regional airlines that GAO interviewed reported difficulties finding sufficient numbers of qualified entry-level first officers. However, mainline airlines, because they hire from the ranks of experienced pilots, have not reported similar concerns, although some mainline airlines expressed concerns that entry-level hiring problems could affect their regional airline partners' ability to provide service to some locations.

Airlines are taking several actions to attract and retain qualified commercial airline pilots. For example, airlines that GAO interviewed have increased recruiting efforts, and developed partnerships with schools to provide incentives and clearer career paths for new pilots. Some regional airlines have offered new first officers signing bonuses or tuition reimbursement to attract more pilots. However, some airlines found these actions insufficient to attract more pilots, and some actions, such as raising wages, have associated costs that have implications for the industry. Airline representatives and pilot schools suggested FAA could do more to give credit for various kinds of flight experience in order to meet the higher flight-hour requirement, and could consider developing alternative pathways to becoming an airline pilot. Stakeholders were also concerned that available financial assistance may not be sufficient, given the high costs of pilot training and relatively low entry-level wages.

ABBREVIATIONS

ATP	airline transport pilot certificate
BLS	Bureau of Labor Statistics
CFI	certified flight instructor
CFR	Code of Federal Regulations
CIP	Classification of Instructional Programs
CPS	Current Population Survey
DOD	Department of Defense
DOL	Department of Labor
DOT	Department of Transportation
Education	Department of Education
ETA	Employment and Training Administration
FAA	Federal Aviation Administration
IPEDS	Integrated Postsecondary Education Data System
MPL	multi-crew pilot license
OES	Occupational Employment Statistics
RACCA	Regional Air Cargo Carriers Association
SOC	Standard Occupational Classification
STEM	science, technology, engineering, and math
R-ATP	restricted-privileges airline transport pilot certificate
VA	Department of Veterans Affairs
WIA	Workforce Investment Act of 1998

February 28, 2014

Congressional Requesters

The airline industry contributes to the U.S. economy by providing global mobility and connectivity in transporting passengers and cargo, as well as significant economic and social benefits to small communities. The U.S. airline industry operated more than 7,000 commercial airplanes in 2012, and there were over 72,000 pilots employed nationwide.[1] Since 2000, the aviation industry has experienced significant turmoil (e.g., the 2001 terrorist attacks, the SARS epidemic, two recessions, and numerous mergers and bankruptcies) that has curtailed its growth. However, recent industry forecasts indicate that the global aviation industry is poised for growth, and airlines around the world, including several domestic airlines that are recalling their remaining furloughed pilots, have announced plans to hire several thousand new pilots in the coming years.

Aviation stakeholders have voiced concerns that an insufficient supply of available and qualified pilots could develop because of imminent retirements, changes to qualification requirements for airline pilots acting as first officers, and perceptions that fewer people are entering pilot schools and fewer pilots exiting the military, among other reasons, thus, challenging airlines' ability to fill the near- and long-term demand for pilots. In light of these stakeholder concerns, you asked us to examine the supply of and demand for airline pilots and potential market and government responses. Specifically, this report describes (1) what the available data and forecasts reveal about the need for and potential availability of airline pilots and (2) the types of industry and government actions that are being taken, or might be taken, to attract and retain airline pilots.[2] To address these objectives, we reviewed economic literature that describes how to evaluate labor market conditions, including identifying a labor shortage.[3] Following the literature, we analyzed data from the Department of Labor's (DOL) Bureau of Labor Statistics' (BLS) Current Population Survey (CPS)—a monthly survey of households conducted by the Bureau of Census for BLS—on the unemployment rate, employment, and median weekly earnings (earnings) from 2000 through 2012. We also obtained data from BLS's Occupational Employment Statistics (OES) survey for employment and wage earnings from 2000 through 2012. These data can be used as indicators of whether labor market conditions are consistent with a shortage. We used SAS, a statistical software application, to connect the BLS CPS data for 2000-2010 and 2011-2012 by the Standard Occupational

Classification (SOC) for aircraft pilots.[4] We analyzed how these indicators have changed over time, and whether these indicators suggest a labor shortage. To verify our results, we consulted with Malcolm Cohen, Ph.D., labor economist and author of the original methodology for conducting indicator analysis, and incorporated his comments as appropriate. We determined the data were sufficiently reliable for the purposes of our indicator analysis to provide context on the labor market. We also reviewed studies that projected the supply of, demand for, or employment for airline pilots. Each study was reviewed by one GAO economist to evaluate its methods, assumptions, and limitations, and this review was then verified by a second GAO economist. For one study, we replicated the analysis using data provided by the lead researchers. We determined these studies were sufficiently reliable for reporting purposes, and where relevant in this report, we described the limitations we identified in these studies. We reviewed data from the Department of Education (Education) on completion rates for degree or certificate programs that might prepare individuals to work as airline pilots; the Department of Defense (DOD) on the number of military pilots leaving the services; and FAA on the numbers of and types of pilot certificates and pilot schools. We also attempted to gather data projections for the next 10 years (2014 through 2023). To understand the extent that employers have had difficulty attracting or retaining airline pilots and whether steps were being taken to mitigate perceived shortages, we interviewed and collected data from various industry stakeholders, including associations representing airlines and airline pilots, mainline and regional airlines,[5] pilot training programs, industry organizations, among others. See appendix I for more information about our scope and methodology and a listing of the stakeholders we interviewed.

We conducted this performance audit from March 2013 through February 2014 in accordance with generally accepted government auditing standards. Those standards require that we plan and perform the audit to obtain sufficient, appropriate evidence to provide a reasonable basis for our findings and conclusions based on our audit objectives. We believe that the evidence obtained provides a reasonable basis for our findings and conclusions based on our audit objectives.

BACKGROUND

The U.S. airline industry is vital to the U.S. economy. Airlines directly generate billions of dollars in revenues each year and contribute to the economic health of the nation. Large and small communities rely on airlines to help connect them to the national transportation system. To operate as an airline carrying passengers or cargo for hire or compensation, a business must have an air carrier (airline) operating certificate issued by the Federal Aviation Administration (FAA), based on federal aviation regulations. Certification is determined by the type of commercial service being provided. Airlines that provide scheduled commercial service operate in accordance with Part 121 of Title 14 of the Code of Federal Regulations (CFR)[6] and are often grouped into two categories: mainline and regional. Mainline airlines include (1) passenger service providers, such as American and Delta that offer domestic and international passenger service on larger airplanes, and (2) cargo service providers, such as United Parcel Service and Federal Express, that offer domestic and international cargo service. Regional airlines include (1) passenger service providers, such as SkyWest and ExpressJet, that offer domestic and limited international passenger service, generally using airplanes with fewer than 90 seats and transporting passengers between large hub airports and smaller airports, and (2) cargo service providers, such as ABX Air and Kalitta Air, that provide domestic and limited international cargo service on a charter or contract basis. Regional airlines generally provide service to smaller communities under capacity purchase agreements[7] with mainline airlines, operate about half of all domestic flights, and carry about 22 percent of all airline passengers. At the end of fiscal year 2012, according to FAA, the U.S. commercial airline industry consisted of 15 scheduled mainline airlines and 70 regional airlines. According to available data, there were over 72,000 airline pilots employed nationwide in 2012. In addition to mainline and regional airlines, other smaller, commercial air-service providers offer scheduled and unscheduled service, via commuter or on-demand operations, and operate in accordance with Part 135 of Title 14 of the CFR.[8]

It takes many years of training and significant financial resources to meet FAA's certification and aeronautical experience qualifications to become an airline pilot. FAA issues several types of pilot certificates that airline pilots progress through—including student pilot, private, commercial, and airline transport pilot (ATP).[9] Federal aviation regulations establish the core requirements for each pilot certification, including the eligibility requirements, aeronautical knowledge, aeronautical experience, and flight proficiency standards. Regulations also govern what pilots with each certificate can do. For example, a private pilot certificate allows pilots to fly solo or carry passengers in any aircraft for which they are qualified, but not to fly for compensation; a commercial pilot certificate is necessary for a variety of non-airline pilot jobs. The ATP certificate is the highest level of pilot certification, requires the highest amount of cumulative flight time and is necessary to fly as a captain or first officer for an airline.

Airline pilots are mostly trained through FAA-certified pilot schools at a college or university—typically through 2- and 4-year degree programs— non-collegiate vocational schools, or in the military. Outside of military training, where service members receive compensation while training to become a pilot, costs can vary significantly for individuals wishing to become a pilot depending on the number of certificates and ratings[10] they wish to attain and the school or training program they choose. Generally, costs to attain a private pilot certificate averages about $9,500, according to the University Aviation Association.[11] However, the academic education and flight training from a 4-year aviation degree program to obtain up to a commercial pilot certificate with additional ratings necessary to be hired as a pilot for commercial flying can cost well in excess of $100,000. Pilot students generally do not come out of collegiate and vocational pilot schools with the necessary requisites to attain an ATP certificate. Individuals will typically graduate from these schools with a commercial pilot certificate, and then they must gain experience by accumulating flight time and pass additional certification testing to obtain an ATP certificate. Similarly, upon separation from the military, military pilots would have to meet the same flight time requirements and pass the certification tests as a civilian pilot would in order to obtain an ATP certificate, although they may be able to use their military flight time to meet those requirements.

Until recently, regional and mainline airlines were permitted to hire first officers who had obtained a commercial pilot certificate which, among other things, required a minimum of 250 hours of flight time.[12] However, following the 2009 Colgan Air, Inc. crash, in New York, the Airline Safety and Federal Aviation Administration Extension Act of 2010[13] mandated that FAA further limit the hours of pilot flight and duty time to combat problems related to pilot fatigue and increase training requirements and pilot qualifications for first officers. In January 2012, FAA issued a rule mandating that pilots have certain rest periods between flights and limiting the number of consecutive hours a pilot may fly.[14] This rule became effective as of January 2014. In July 2013, FAA, as required by the law, issued a new pilot qualification rule that increased the requirements for first officers who can fly for U.S. passenger and cargo airlines.[15] The rule requires that first officers now hold an ATP certificate, just as captains must hold, requiring, among other things, a minimum of 1,500 hours of total time as a pilot.[16] The law also gave FAA discretion to allow specific academic training courses to be credited toward the required hours of total time as a pilot.[17] As such, the rule included an allowance for pilots with fewer than 1,500 hours of total time as a pilot to obtain a "restricted-privileges" ATP certificate (R-ATP)—that is, to allow pilots to serve as first officers until they obtain the necessary 1,500 hours of total time as a pilot needed for an ATP certificate—when they meet certain requirements[18] and are:

1) former military pilots with 750 hours of total time as a pilot;
2) graduates of approved 4-year aviation degree programs with 1,000 hours of total time as a pilot and meet other requirements;[19] or
3) graduates of approved 2-year aviation degree programs with 1,250 hours of total time as a pilot and meet other requirements. [20]

As of January 24, 2014, 37 collegiate 2- and 4-year aviation degree programs have been authorized to certify graduates to be eligible to apply for an R-ATP certificate.

Although previously permitted to hire first officers with commercial pilot certificates, mainline airlines have generally required their first officers to possess an ATP certificate. Regional airlines, however, would frequently hire entry-level pilots as first officers who had completed training in collegiate and vocational pilot schools and held a commercial pilot certificate and an instrument rating[21] after these individuals had gained additional aeronautical experience. Previously these graduates could work as first officers for regional airlines and build the additional flight time necessary to qualify for an ATP certificate, but under the new pilot qualification rule, they must attain this experience in other ways prior to being eligible to fly for a regional airline. As a result, FAA and industry stakeholders estimate it may take an additional 1-2 years for pilots coming out of school (roughly 6 years or more from the beginning of training) to accrue the required number of flight hours to qualify for an ATP certificate.[22] Options available to these pilots to build the necessary flight hours include:

- Obtain a certified flight instructor (CFI) certificate which allows pilots to accrue flight hours while instructing new student pilots. [23]
- Become employed with Part 135 air service providers (i.e., commuter and on-demand, or non-Part 121 cargo operations) as a first officer, where a commercial pilot certificate (minimum 250 hours) is required, among other requirements.

- Become employed performing Part 91 operations—such as banner towing, crop dusting, and corporate flights.[24]
- Pay for flight time such as renting aircraft for flying or training in a flight simulation training device.[25]
- Work abroad for foreign airlines, or join the U.S. military and be trained as a pilot.

Several federal agencies have a role in supporting and developing the pilot workforce. As mentioned, FAA is responsible for the administration of pilot certification (licensing), among other things, and DOD, the Department of Veterans Affairs (VA), DOL and its Employment and Training Administration (ETA), and Education each have a role that may contribute to the availability of airline pilots (see table 1).

Table 1. Federal Roles and Responsibilities for Pilot Certification and Funding Aviation Training

Agency	Role
FAA	FAA issues pilot certificates and ratings; sets requirements and oversees the training provided by FAA-approved collegiate and non-collegiate vocational pilot schools and testing; sets and enforces regulations for airline operations, including crew requirements.
DOD/VA	U.S. airlines have historically recruited pilots trained in the U.S. military service branches. DOD also provides educational assistance to service members to help them enhance their professional development, which can be usedfor pilot training. VA also administers education benefit programs that can be used to pay for flight training for veterans who are interested in attending approved aviation programs.
DOL/ETA/BLS	DOL-supported workforce-training services can be used to fund aviation training. BLS collects employment and wagedata and develops long-term (10-year) employment projections.
Education	Education provides financial assistance to support training in aviation-related fields.

Source: GAO analysis of government information.

Over the last decade, the civil aviation industry has been volatile because demand for air travel is sensitive to the state of the economy as well as to political, international, and even health-related events. As a result, despite periods of strong growth and earnings, the industry has at times suffered substantial financial distress resulting in the industry's contraction. For example, in response to the 2007-2009 economic recession and resulting decrease in demand for commercial air travel, airlines cut capacity, downsized their fleets, and reduced their workforce. However, as demand for air travel has rebounded and is expected to grow, airlines are now looking to hire a substantial number of pilots. Further, the U.S. airline industry is concerned there will not be a sufficient number of qualified airline pilots to support this growth and a labor shortage will result. While no agreed-upon definition for a labor shortage exists, it is commonly described as a sustained period during which the demand for workers exceeds the supply of workers available and willing to work at a particular wage and in specific working conditions at a particular place.[26]

DATA ARE MIXED REGARDING THE EXTENT OF AN AIRLINE PILOT SHORTAGE, BUT REGIONAL AIRLINES ARE EXPERIENCING DIFFICULTIES HIRING ENTRY-LEVEL PILOTS

Historical labor market data from 2000 through 2012 provide mixed evidence as to whether an airline pilot shortage exists. The unemployment rate for the pilot occupation—a key indicator for a shortage—has been much lower than for the economy as a whole, which is consistent with a shortage. On the other hand, wage earnings and employment were not consistent with the existence of a shortage, as data for both indicators showed decreases over the period. In looking forward, to meet the expectation of growth in the industry and to replace expected mandatory age-related pilot retirements, projections indicate the industry will need to hire a few thousand pilots on average each year over the next 10 years. Data indicate that a large pool of qualified pilots exists relative to the projected demand, but whether such pilots are willing or available to work at wages being offered is unknown. Furthermore, the number of pilot certificate holders has not been increasing, and fewer students are entering and completing collegiate pilot training programs. Studies and analyses related to the supply of airline pilots find that a shortage may arise depending on several factors, including the extent of future industry growth, the wages being offered, and escalation in education costs. As airlines have started hiring to address growth demands and attrition, 11 of the 12 regional airlines we interviewed reported difficulties filling entry-level first-officer vacancies. Mainline airlines, since they hire experienced pilots largely from regional airlines, have not reported similar difficulties, although mainline airline representatives expressed concerns that entry-level hiring problems could affect the ability of their regional partners to provide service to some locations.

Some Historical Labor Market Data Are Consistent with the Presence of a Pilot Shortage, and Other Data Are Not

While no single metric can be used to identify whether a labor shortage exists, labor market data can be used as "indicators," in conjunction with observations from stakeholders.[27] According to economic literature, one can look at historical unemployment rates, as well as trends in employment and earnings.[28] If a labor shortage were to exist, one would expect (1) a low unemployment rate signaling limited availability of workers in a profession, (2) increases in employment due to increased demand for that occupation, and (3) increases in wages offered to draw more people into the industry.[29] Of these three indicators, the unemployment rate provides the most direct measure of a labor shortage because it estimates the number of people who are unemployed and actively looking for work in a specific occupation.[30] The BLS household survey-based CPS data used to evaluate these three indicators combined airline and commercial pilots into a single occupational category of pilots; therefore, we cannot isolate the extent to which the indicators apply to only airline pilots, although airline pilots represent about two-thirds of the employment within the occupation.[31]

According to BLS data we analyzed from 2000 through 2012, the unemployment rate of pilots has averaged 2.7 percent—a much lower unemployment rate than for the economy as a whole.[32] This level of unemployment would be consistent with a shortage because it suggests few pilots during this time frame reported that they were looking for employment as a pilot and were unable to find it. Furthermore, in relative terms, over the entire period, the pilot occupation had the 53rd lowest unemployment rate out of the 295 occupations for which annual BLS data is available.

Data on the other two indicators, wage earnings and employment growth, are not consistent with the existence of a shortage in the occupation. First, our analysis of BLS data from 2000 through 2012 shows that the median weekly earnings in the pilot occupation decreased by 9.5 percent over the period (adjusted for inflation), or by an average of 0.8 percent per year.[33] According to economic literature, a positive growth in wages is required for a shortage to be present. So, by absolute standards, the findings for this indicator do not appear consistent with a shortage for pilots during the time frame.[34] We also compared wages in this occupation to all other occupations and found wage growth for pilots has been low compared to other occupations. Specifically, the pilot occupation would be 187th out of the 250 occupations for which annual data are available. However, other factors can account for a decline or lack of growth in earnings even during a labor shortage. Earnings may be slow to adjust to other labor market trends, or certain aspects of an industry may prevent wages from increasing. For example, airlines may have limited flexibility to adjust wages for entry-level positions in response to a potential shortage due to seniority-based airlines' pay systems in place for pilots and because airlines' pilot wages are often negotiated contractually with labor unions.

Second, for the rate of employment growth, our analysis showed employment for pilots has actually decreased by 12 percent from 2000 to 2012, a decrease that is also not consistent with a shortage.[35] As previously stated, the airline industry has experienced considerable volatility over the last decade due to recessions, bankruptcies, and merger and acquisition activities that have curtailed growth in the industry. By relative standards, the rate of employment growth for the pilot occupation ranked about 331st of the 490 occupations for which annual BLS data is available.

Our analysis of labor market data has a number of limitations given the nature of the CPS and OES data from BLS and the scope of our analysis. Occupations in the SOC system are classified using occupational definitions that describe the work performed and may not take into account specific requirements an employer seeks. For example, some airlines may require specific aircraft type ratings.[36] We identified the following other limitations of the labor market indicators:

- Data are collected through a household survey and are subject to sampling and response errors. Typically, one individual will identify occupation, employment, and wage data for all household members; individuals may report incorrect or inconsistent information.
- Survey results of unemployment rates are based on the person's last job, rather than the longest job held or occupation in which a person is trained or looking for work; the data therefore can miss individuals who are seeking work in a particular occupation. For example, airline pilots who lost their jobs, worked temporarily in another occupation

(perhaps even within aviation), but considered themselves pilots and were seeking employment as pilots when surveyed would not be counted as unemployed pilots in the CPS data; rather, they would be classified according to the occupation they had held temporarily.

- BLS collects data on earnings for pilots in all stages of their careers, so we could not examine whether starting earnings—which would be more likely to indicate if wages were rising to attract entry-level workers—have increased.
- Data are collected at a national level; while not all indicators were consistent with a labor shortage, our analysis would not identify any regional shortages.
- Research by BLS and others suggests job vacancy data as another potential indicator for identifying labor shortages. However, BLS does not collect information on job vacancies at the occupational level. Some job vacancy data are collected by some states and private companies, but the data are limited. We could not obtain complete and sufficiently reliable occupational-level job-vacancy data from these sources.[37]

Finally, as mentioned above, no single measure can provide definitive evidence as to whether a labor shortage exists. Rather, these data can indicate the extent to which employers may have difficulty attracting people at the current wage rate. Moreover, even if perfect data existed, the term "labor shortage" is sometimes used to describe a variety of situations, some of which are generally not considered to be shortages.[38] For example, during periods of economic recession, employers may become accustomed to hiring a high caliber of candidate with specific training or levels of experience at a prescribed wage rate. In these cases, employers can be more selective when hiring from among the candidates for the position. However, during an economic expansion, when companies may be increasing the size of their workforce, it is likely that the number of job applicants will shrink and employers may have difficulty finding the same caliber of candidates that they could find during a downturn. Under these circumstances the employer's challenge may become one of quality of available people, not necessarily quantity of people willing and able to do the job. Economic literature also suggests that to describe the nature and scope of any potential shortage, these indicators should be considered in conjunction with other information, such as trends in the industry that can affect the demand of and supply for qualified professionals and the hiring experiences of employers, which we discuss in the following sections.

Projected Employment Growth and Retirements Suggest the Need for an Average of a Few Thousand New Pilots a Year over the Next Decade

The number of pilots that U.S. airlines will need to hire will be driven by increases in passenger traffic (growth) and replacements for retiring and attriting pilots. Several reports have projected the need for pilots in the future. Audries Aircraft Analysis—an aviation industry analysis firm— developed a forecast of pilot needs over the next 10 years based on forecasts of new aircraft orders and expected deliveries from aircraft manufacturers Boeing, Airbus, and Embraer.[39] Using industry averages for numbers of pilots needed per plane, the forecast determines how many pilots will be needed to accommodate the projected fleet growth, and couples this number with industry data regarding expected retirements. An academic study conducted by researchers from six universities, led by researchers from the University of North Dakota, forecasts the demand for pilots using similar techniques.[40] FAA also projects the need for pilots based on forecasts of growth in passenger demand and expected retirements. While these projections are helpful in gaining a sense for potential changes in aviation employment, developing long-term occupational employment projections is inherently uncertain for a variety of reasons. Most importantly, each projection relies on a set of assumptions about the future, some of which may not come to fruition. For example, the projections discussed above relied on assumptions of continued economic growth, but if a recession or other unexpected economic event were to occur, the projections for employment are likely to be overstated.[41] These projections vary in their results and based on those results, we estimated that a range of roughly 1,900 to 4,500 new pilots will be needed to be hired on average annually over the next 10 years, as follows:

- **Audries Aircraft Analysis** developed pilot demand forecasts based on aircraft manufacturers' forecasts of fleet growth. Each manufacturer uses a slightly different method to create its forecasts. For example, some projections include certain cargo aircraft, and some do not. Despite the differences in methods, the fleet growth forecasts yielded similar results. Each forecast resulted in the projected need for pilots steadily rising over the next 10 years to accommodate growth and replacement of retiring and attriting pilots. Annually averaged, the Embraer forecast resulted in a projection of about 2,900 new pilots needed per year over the next decade; the Boeing forecast resulted in about 3,300 new pilots, and the Airbus forecast resulted in about 3,900 new pilots. It is important to note that these forecasts encompass the entire North American market and are not specific to the United States. In addition, the Boeing forecast projected demand for 498,000 new airline pilots worldwide over the next 20 years. The effect of this global demand for pilots may also have an effect on the available supply of pilots for U.S. airlines in the future, as foreign airlines also recruit U.S. pilots.

- **Academic study led by the University of North Dakota** estimated demand for pilots for roughly the next 20 years in its study of airline pilot labor supply. This study derived demand based on industry growth, retirements, and attrition for reasons other than retirements. Industry growth was derived from forecasts of new aircraft from the Airline Monitor[42] and estimates of the average number of pilots needed per aircraft. Expected retirements came from industry data, and the study used an estimate of an attrition rate for reasons other than retirement of 1.5 percent. The study estimates that the industry would need to hire over 95,000 new pilots over about the next 20 years, with about 45,000 being needed in the next 10 years, for an annual average of about 4,500 over the next decade.

- **FAA 2013 forecast** projects that passenger demand for U.S. airlines over the next 20 years will grow at an average 2.2 percent per year through 2033, with slow or no growth expected in 2013 and slight growth over the next 5 years assuming the U.S. economy grows at a faster rate.[43] To account for this industry growth and to replace retiring pilots, FAA projects that about 70,000 new pilots with an ATP certificate through 2032 will be needed.[44] This equates to an average need for about 3,400 new pilots annually over the next 10 years.

- **BLS Employment Projections 2012–2022** assumes a 6.6 percent net decrease in employment in the overall number of airline pilot positions through the year 2022—which equated to about 4,400 fewer pilot jobs over the time period. This is in contrast with the average expected occupational growth of 10.8 percent for all occupations for this period. Based on the employment projection, we calculated that an average of 440 pilot jobs will be lost annually through 2022. However, while fewer airline pilot jobs will exist during the 10-year period, BLS also projects, at the same time, 19,200 airline pilot job openings, or an annual average of 1,920 openings, that may be available to be filled due to retirements and attrition. The BLS employment projections assume that growth in supply will be adequate to meet the demand, and so the analysis is not designed to forecast whether a labor shortage might develop in any given occupation.

In addition to the need for airlines to hire new pilots based on industry growth and replacement of retirements, FAA's new rule on pilot flight and duty time may engender a one-time staffing adjustment for airlines. Current crew schedules can vary by airline, the labor contract involved, and the number of pilots assigned to operate each aircraft, and airlines we interviewed varied in their estimates of how many additional pilots they would be need to meet the new requirements. Airlines' estimates ranged from no effect on the number of pilots needed to 15 percent increase in the number of pilots needed as of January 2014.

While these projections suggest the need for between roughly 1,900 and 4,500 new pilots on an average annual basis over the next 10 years, we cannot indicate with any level of certainty the actual number of new airline pilots that will be needed or hired in the future. Airlines make a variety of business decisions to meet passenger demand for airlines' operations that could affect the number of pilots that the airlines would need or are able to hire. According to information provided by eight mainline airlines, they expect to hire about 20,800 new pilots from 2014 through 2023. Accordingly, several mainline airlines have announced plans to recall all of their remaining furloughed pilots or begin new hiring efforts. For example, in September 2013, United issued recall notices to its remaining 600 furloughed pilots. According to United representatives, it has also started hiring new pilots with an initial goal of about 60 pilots a month to address the airline's projected future needs. While American and Delta had already recalled all of their furloughed pilots, each announced plans for future hiring. In October 2013, American announced plans to hire 1,500 pilots over 5 years. Delta planned to hire 300 pilots in November 2013 and expects to hire about 50 pilots per month through September 2014. Several regional airlines we spoke to have also been actively hiring new pilots. For example, since March 2013, ExpressJet has hired from

32 to 48 pilots monthly. Also, representatives of American Eagle told us that they expect to hire an average of 250 pilots per year for the next 10 years.

Data and Studies of Pilot Supply Provide Some Evidence of the Potential for a Shortage to Emerge

Pools of Certificate Holders Are Large Relative to Employment, but Are Not Increasing

While there were over 72,000 airline pilots employed in 2012, FAA data show a total of 137,658 active pilots under the age of 65 who held ATP certificates, as of January 6, 2014.[45] This large pool of ATP certificate holders, however, can include pilots who are not available for work or are not suitable or competent to act as pilots in airline operations on large jet-powered aircraft. Data were not available to determine or verify how many active ATP certificate holders were otherwise employed. The pilots not employed by airlines may also be serving as pilots in the U.S. military, employed as pilots in non-airline operations, employed by foreign airlines, employed in non-pilot jobs in the aviation industry, or working in non-aviation careers. With respect to pilots holding FAA pilot certificates and potentially working for foreign airlines, in 2012 according to FAA data, about 7,858 pilots with ATP certificates (or about 5 percent of the total number of pilots with ATP certificates) and about 15,994 pilots with commercial certificates (or about14 percent of the total number of pilots with commercial pilot certificates) are listed with a documented residence outside of the United States.

In addition to ATP certificate holders, a large population of commercial pilot certificate holders with instrument ratings also exists. In 2012, for instance, a total of over 116,000 pilots held commercial pilot certificates and about 105,000 of these pilots also held an instrument rating. While not currently qualified to be airline pilots, future ATP certificate holders typically come from this pool, and the instrument ratings held by some of these individuals suggest that they may be on a pathway to qualifying for an ATP certificate. According to FAA officials, the number of pilots holding an instrument rating is a good indicator for forecasting pilots who are more likely to seek an ATP certificate because an instrument rating is a requirement of ATP certification; an instrument rating is not, however, a requirement to hold a commercial pilot certificate.[46]

While these pools of existing ATP and commercial pilot certificate holders exist, the pools have remained relatively flat since 2000 (see fig. 1).

- The number of pilots under age 65 holding active ATP certificates decreased about 1 percent from 2000 through 2012, while the number of new certificates issued annually decreased 17 percent during this period (7,715 to 6,396) (see fig. 2). However, new issuance of ATP certificates has increased since 2010, an increase that would be expected given that the new pilot qualification rule took effect in July 2013.

- Commercial pilot certificate holders under age 65 increased 4 percent from 2000 through 2012. The number of new certificates issued each year averaged about 9,900 over this time period.[47]

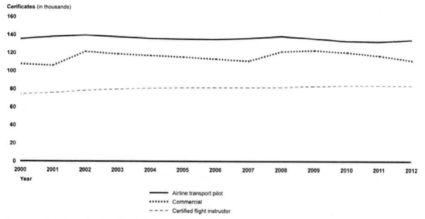

Source: GAO analysis of FAA data.
Note: Our study concerns airline pilots. We excluded all pilots who were 65 years and older because U.S. law requires airline pilots to retire at age 65.

Figure 1. Number of U.S. Pilot Certificates Held by Type for Pilots under Age 65 from 2000 through 2012.

We note that these populations of pilots holding active commercial and ATP certificates, while currently relatively large, have been larger in the past. Also, when mainline airlines increase pilot hiring, the rate at which new pilots enter the pipeline would likely increase, as would the rate at which pilots holding commercial pilot certificates upgrade to ATP certificates. To illustrate, from 1990 through 2000, mainline airlines hired about 31,300 pilots.[48] During that period, the number of ATP certificates held increased by roughly the same number—from 107,732 to 141,596— while the number of commercial pilot certificates held also decreased by roughly the same amount—from 149,666 to

121,858. In contrast, when hiring slowed from 2001 through 2012 and mainline airlines hired about 16,900 pilots, there was a decrease in the total number of airline pilot jobs and the number of ATP certificates held increased only slightly—from 144,702 to 145,590—while the number of commercial pilot certificates held actually decreased—from 120,502 to 116,400. The average number of new commercial pilots certificates issued each year was also lower in this period (9,780) compared to the 1990's (11,688).

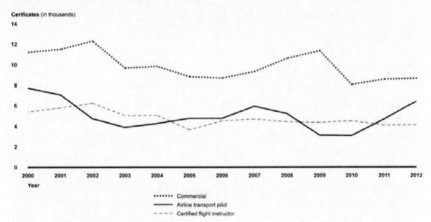

Source: GAO analysis of FAA data.

Figure 2. Number of New U.S. Pilot Certificates Issued by Type from 2000 through 2012.

The number of flight instructors is another predictor of individuals moving through the pipeline to becoming an airline pilot. The number of pilots under age 65 holding active flight instructor certificates increased 13 percent from 2000 through 2012 (see fig. 1), while the number of new flight instructor certificates issued each year averaged about 4,700 over this period and remained relatively flat (see fig. 2). Under the new pilot qualification rule, aspiring pilots must accrue more flight hours than was the case in the past, and stakeholders expect that flight instruction is likely to be one of the primary means of attaining these hours. This means that new pilot graduates who decide to work as flight instructors to gain hours will need to hold such positions for a longer period of time. If this occurs, flight instructor turnover will be slower and new pilot graduates may have more difficulty finding flight instructor positions. On the other hand, representatives of three of the pilot schools we spoke to told us that they are currently facing a shortage of qualified flight instructors.

Enrollments in and Graduations from Pilot Programs Appear to Be Declining

Available evidence suggests that fewer students are entering and completing pilot training since 2001. According to Education's data, the cumulative number of graduates (completions) of undergraduate professional pilot-degree programs—those most likely to pursue a career as an airline pilot—decreased about 23 percent from academic years 2000-2001 through 2011-2012 (see fig. 3).[49] Although data on enrollments are not available, representatives from most of the collegiate and vocational pilot schools we interviewed told us their schools have experienced declines in undergraduate enrollments over the last 10 years.[50] Further, representatives of the 10 collegiate aviation and 2 non-collegiate vocational pilot schools reported waning interest among current and prospective students wanting to pursue professional pilot education.

According to these representatives, the airline pilot career has lost some of its historical appeal for young people over the last 10 years due to a variety of factors, including increases in education costs, limited sources of financial assistance, negative perceptions of working conditions and wages for new pilots, and a perceived lack of stability in the industry. In addition, according to these representatives, the new first officer qualification requirements have also had some impact on student perceptions.

The new requirements mean pilots must spend additional time accruing flight hours (i.e., 1-2 additional years) prior to being qualified to apply to an airline, during the time when new pilots may be receiving relatively low wages (for example, according to the Aircraft Owners and Pilots Association, flight instructors typically make less than $20,000 per year),[51] and students are facing a longer period of time before they will be financially able to begin repaying their student loan debt. As a result, according to recruiters from four of the schools, students' parents are less encouraging of the career. According to officials at three collegiate aviation schools, due to these and other factors, more students interested in working in the aviation industry are pursuing other piloting careers, such as in unmanned aircraft systems. To illustrate, the officials said that in 2012, they sampled 240 new flight instructor pilots at 17 different collegiate aviation schools and found that while 69 percent (166 instructors) responded that they initially aspired to be airline pilots when they started their pilot training education, only about 38 percent (91 instructors) had aspirations to be airline pilots after graduating from training. Representatives of 5 collegiate aviation and 2 non-collegiate vocational pilot schools also reported financial hardships for many students enrolled in pilot education. Officials representing two collegiate schools told us that based on their discussions with students dropping out of professional pilot education, the lack of financial resources or assistance is often a barrier for students.

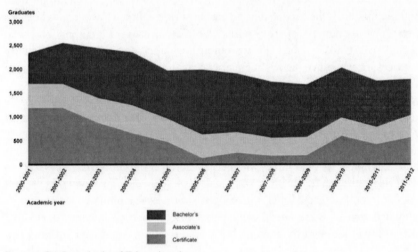

Source: GAO analysis of Education data.
Note: The year shown is the end of the academic year. For example, 2001 encompasses the 2000- 2001 school year.

Figure 3. Number of Graduates from U.S. Collegiate Professional-Pilot Programs by Degree Type, from Academic Years 2001 through 2012.

Former Military Pilots Are No Longer a Significant Supply Source

Although historically, the military has been a significant source of pilots for the airlines, according to some airline industry representatives we interviewed, the number of former military pilots being hired by airlines has been declining. According to these representatives, prior to 2001, some 70 percent of airline pilots hired came from the military, whereas currently they estimated roughly 30 percent come from the military. In addition, all of the airlines we interviewed reported that fewer candidates with military experience are applying for pilot job vacancies than has been their experience in the past. While specific data are not available on the number of pilots separating from the military who sought and gained employment at airlines, according to DOD data, from fiscal years 2001 through 2012, an average of

2,400 pilots separated from the military service branches per year.[52] DOD expects roughly the same trend to continue into the foreseeable future, although future trends may be influenced by several factors, including financial incentives to influence pilots to stay in the military longer, civil job market opportunities, and changing post-war military missions. Once separated from the military, these pilots could choose to seek employment at an airline if FAA pilot certification requirements are met, such as flight hour minimums and other requisites, to be an airline pilot. However, we cannot determine the number of these pilots who may meet these qualifications, who would seek employment with civilian airlines after exiting from the military services, or who have the flight experience that airlines require.

Studies and Analyses of Pilot Supply Trends Find that the Extent of any Shortage Depends on Changes in Wages, Industry Growth, and Education Costs

We identified and reviewed three studies that examined pilot supply trends and attempted to determine whether a shortage of pilots may arise given expected retirements, attrition, and increases in demand. Two analyses of pilot supply trends suggested that a prolonged shortage was unlikely to develop, [53] although one of these specifically noted that a shortage of entry-level first officers may temporarily emerge, but would likely be addressed within a few years. This same analysis—conducted by the MITRE Corporation—found that, similar to our earlier discussion, a large pool of pilots with lower level pilot certificates exists in the United States who would be available to obtain the higher ATP certification if demand were to increase.[54] The study also noted that there is a significant pool of trained pilots employed outside the United States or in the military that could be drawn from to fill airline vacancies. However, avoiding a shortage would hinge on the ability to incent lower level pilots to seek a higher certification, and to incent pilots currently working abroad or elsewhere into U.S. airline jobs, should a shortage arise. Both analyses state or imply that airlines may need to provide financial incentives—for example, higher wages, benefits, or bonuses—to bring new pilots into the industry. While such actions would be considered typical market responses to a potential shortage, it does not mean such actions are costless or might not have implications for the industry.

The academic study led by the University of North Dakota, which was discussed previously, concluded that U.S. airlines will experience a cumulative shortage of about 35,000 pilots over the next 20 years if no actions are taken by the airline industry or government.[55]

Using regression analysis, the study found that the number of new CFI certifications has a positive association with pilot hiring by mainline airlines—that is, as pilot hiring tends to increase so do new CFI certifications; however, it has a negative association with the cost of pilot school—that is, as educational costs increase, new CFI certifications tend to decrease. Because of the significant finding of a potential shortage, we reviewed the study's methodology.

We also replicated the study's analysis to better understand how the study's key assumptions affected its results. We found that the study's findings of a shortage were based on expectations of hiring needs of mainline airlines of about 95,000 pilots over the next 20 years,[56] and the supply of new pilots being curtailed by the continued acceleration in the cost of training, relative to the general rate of inflation.

To predict future excess cost growth (the increase in the cost of pilot training over and above the general economy-wide level of inflation), the study extrapolated the growth of inflation in the cost of flight training over the past several years to the next 20 years. While using historic trends to predict future changes is part of forecasting, in some cases, it can lead to results that may be unlikely.[57] In this case, this method resulted in forecasted year-over-year changes in the cost of flight school of almost 8 percent above its historic mean by the year 2030, which is well above historic averages over the past 20 years. However, other changes in the market for pilot training, such as the openings of other pilot schools, for example, could reduce this inflation. Using a different assumption regarding increases in training costs would result in different outcomes with respect to the size of the forecasted shortage. In fact, guidance from the Office of Management and Budget suggests that assumptions regarding price increases (such as the continuation of current trends) should be varied to test the sensitivity of the final results to that assumption. For example, we found that reducing the assumed rate of increase of inflation in the cost of flight training to only 1-2 points above its historic mean resulted in about 30,000 more CFI certifications—largely ameliorating the estimated shortage.

However, the researchers stated that they felt that extrapolating from current trends would be the most responsible forecast to consider but agreed that if the costs of training do not continue to increase at an escalating rate, relative to inflation, as the study forecasted, then the estimated shortage of pilots could be mitigated.

Regional Airlines Report Difficulties Filling Entry-Level Vacancies

Representatives at 11 of the 12 regional airlines told us they have been unable to meet hiring targets for training classes for new-hire first officers; most reported since early 2013. In anticipation of the August 2013 deadline for the new pilot qualification rule, officials at many of these airlines indicated that 6 to 12 months before this deadline, they began seeking new pilots to hire who already had an ATP certificate or had enough flight hours that additional flying would allow them to reach the minimum to qualify for an ATP certificate by the time FAA finalized the rule. However, representatives of 5 regional airlines indicated they have generally been able to meet about 50 percent of their hiring targets to fill training classes. For example, one regional airline representative told us that his airline had monthly targets of hiring 12 new pilots from August through October 2013 but has been able to hire from 2 to 6 qualified applicants each month. Representatives of most of the regional airlines also reported that their existing banks of qualified pilot applicants have dwindled and that they receive fewer applicants than they have had historically in response to hiring announcements. Representatives of one regional airline estimated that where they may have previously had over 1,000 applicants for hiring announcements, they are now seeing about 100. For the most part, as a result of the new pilot qualification rule, many of the representatives attributed this reduction in the number of applicants to a couple of factors. First, fewer overall number of applicants are available who can meet ATP requirements. Second, according to several of the representatives, pilots completing training from pilot schools must now spend more time accruing required flight time— and forego some potential career earnings—before they can apply for entry-level first-officer jobs at regional airlines, and fewer jobs are available in general aviation and non-airline commercial sectors for pilots to accrue the needed flight hours. Additionally, representatives of 6 regional airlines noted that increasing numbers of applicants were not showing up for scheduled interviews; some of the representatives speculated that this might be due to opportunities at other regional airlines or other jobs.

Representatives at 10 of the 12 regional airlines we interviewed told us they have also observed an overall decline in the quality of flight experience of qualified pilots applying for pilot jobs, while some cited higher drop-out rates among new hire classes or observed that new hire candidates seem to be less prepared for the airline environment, compared to the historic norm. Prior to the new pilot qualification rule, regional airlines would often hire entry-level pilots who had recently graduated from pilot training with a commercial pilot certificate and an instrument rating, and had gained between 500 and 700 hours of flight time in commercial operations or in flight instruction.[58] The pilot would then be hired at the regional airline, enter training with the airline, and accrue flight time experience towards an ATP certificate in the airline environment. According to representatives from most of the regional airlines, as a result of the new pilot qualification rule, future applicants will have had to accrue an additional 500 to 750 hours of flight time in flight instruction, where they are not always actually flying a plane, or operating in the general aviation (Part 91) environment wherein flight time is accrued in aircraft such as small, single- and multiengine, propeller airplanes that are not as technically advanced as aircraft operated by airlines. According to these representatives, in their experience, applicants with the greater number of flight hours earned outside the airline environment were less proficient and prepared than previous applicants who had recently completed pilot training with between 500 and 700 hours of flight time. While this has been the recent experience of some regional airlines, we do not have data on where aspiring airline pilots are gaining their flight experience, or empirical evidence regarding how this has changed since the new pilot qualification rule went into effect. Furthermore, judgment on what type of flight experience is most suitable for would-be airline pilots is outside the scope of this report.

Representatives at most of the regional airlines also noted that some of the difficulty in finding sufficient numbers of pilots with ATP certificates, being experienced by some regional airlines, could be influenced by current perceptions about the potential for career opportunities and progression. Key factors that influence pilots to pursue a job with an airline include the opportunity for upgrading to a captain, type of equipment flown, and work schedule. Pilots' pay rates at airlines are based on seniority with a particular airline, and the rates increase each year and when pilots progress from first officer to captain. According to available data for 14 regional airlines, the average new hire hourly wage for all airplane types is currently about $24 per hour for the first year of employment.[59] However, representatives of most of the regional airlines said the hourly wages increase for the second year of employment for first officers—to about $30, according to the data for the 14 airlines. Regional airlines generally tend to have newer pilots who accumulate flight time in smaller aircraft and use that experience as a stepping stone to the higher wages offered at mainline airlines.

According to FAA, the reason that regional airline first officers are willing to accept a relatively low initial salary is because of the increases in salary that come later in the career, when they advance sequentially to regional airline captain, mainline airline first officer, and, finally, mainline airline captain. 60 The average number of years to upgrade from first officer to captain is 5 years for regional airlines, but representatives of several regional airlines said they expected upgrades to take longer. In addition, the new pilot qualification rule have extended the period before a pilot can be hired by an airline. Therefore, individuals interested in an airline pilot career would likely expect several more years at the lower end of the pay scale than had been the case in the past. Several industry representatives also noted, however, that the potential career earnings for an airline pilot continue to be significant. Some senior captains at mainline airlines can make $200,000 or more annually in base salary.

Pilot pay rates are also based on the type of aircraft that airlines fly because higher pay rates are associated with flying larger, more complex airplanes, and, thus, opportunities to eventually upgrade to flying these airplanes are important in progressing in the career. Representatives of 6 of the 12 regional airlines generally said that young, entry-level pilots have tended to favor the airlines that operate larger regional jet airplanes as opposed to those that operate turboprop-powered airplanes. Therefore, according to one regional airline, it could be difficult at times for some regional airlines to find pilots to hire as first officers willing to fly, for example, small turboprop airplanes when other opportunities are available with other airlines to immediately or eventually fly larger regional jets due to the career opportunities and associated higher pay rates. According to two small regional airlines—those that generally operate small turboprop airplanes—previous to the new pilot qualification rule, they were able to attract sufficient numbers of pilots with an expectation that these pilots would build flight experience over several years and eventually leave for other airline opportunities. However, since the rule went into effect, small regional airlines of this size cannot compete for the available pilots with ATP certificates. Due to issues in finding enough pilots with ATP certificates, one of these small regional airlines has petitioned FAA for approval that would allow it to use some of its smaller 19-seat airplanes under a Part 135 operation—which would not be subject to the new first-officer qualification requirement to have an ATP certificate—on specific routes.[61]

According to the representatives of the mainline airlines we spoke with, they are not currently experiencing any difficulty in attracting qualified and desirable candidates. These representatives generally credited higher pay and benefits, better retirement options, and more flexible work schedules than what regional airlines typically offer. For instance, the average hourly wage for first officers at 10 mainline airlines for all airplane types, for which an ATP certificate is required, is currently about $48 per hour for the first year of employment. The mainline airline representatives did not anticipate any problems as they seek to increase hiring in the future and stated that they could draw from the pool of pilots now employed at regional airlines. However, representatives did express concerns that their regional partners may be experiencing difficulties finding qualified entry-level pilots. Representatives at two mainline airlines were concerned that as they pull pilots from the ranks of their regional partners, the regional partners may have trouble replacing those pilots, a potential chain reaction that might result in regional connecting services' being curtailed. Five regional airlines we interviewed are currently limiting service to some smaller communities because they did not have pilots available to provide that service. Other industry stakeholders expressed similar concerns that service to small communities will continue to suffer going forward.

INDUSTRY AND GOVERNMENT ARE TAKING SOME ACTIONS TO ATTRACT AND TRAIN FUTURE PILOTS

Economic literature identifies possible actions that employers in a market may take to mitigate a labor shortage. Some of the actions discussed in economic literature are already occurring as part of airline, collegiate pilot school, and government efforts to attract more pilots to the airline industry, including increased recruiting and financial incentives. However, such actions have associated costs and can affect the industry in various ways. Federal agencies have several programs aimed at promoting aviation careers and providing financial assistance for education. However, stakeholders suggested several additional actions that government could take to increase the availability and flexibility of financial assistance available to pilot students and to create additional pathways to becoming an airline pilot.

The Aviation Industry Has Taken Various Steps to Attract, Train, and Retain Airline Pilots

According to economic literature we reviewed, employers—which are the first to identify a shortage when they encounter difficulty filling vacancies at the current wage rate—may take several actions in response to a perceived labor shortage.[62] The actions vary in desirability for the employer based on resources required and their permanency. For example, increasing recruiting requires fewer resources than raising wages; further recruitment efforts could also be halted if labor market conditions change, whereas wages, once raised, may not be easily lowered. Employers may also choose to take some of these actions for reasons other than filling vacancies—for instance, to improve morale among current employees or to increase profitability. Some of the actions suggested in the literature are not feasible for airlines to take with respect to pilots.[63]

In response to difficulties filling employment vacancies, employers may:

- *Increase recruiting efforts.* This includes such activities as increasing advertising, using public or private employment agencies, and paying recruiting bonuses to employees who refer new hires.
- *Train workers for the job.* In a difficult labor market, an employer that traditionally relied upon colleges or vocational or trade schools to train its workforce may choose to offer or sponsor training.
- *Improve working conditions.* Equipment or facility upgrades, training, and job recognition efforts may all be effective means to attract and retain personnel.
- *Reduce the minimum qualifications for the job.* Employers may have set minimum qualifications higher than necessary and may choose to reduce those qualifications when hiring becomes difficult. As discussed, regulation sets minimum qualifications for airline pilots. However, most regional and mainline airlines could have hiring requirements in excess of or addition to the regulatory minimums that could be reduced, although airlines with such requirements are often not willing to do so because they view their requirements as important to the safe operation of their airline.
- *Offer bonuses to new employees.* Employers may offer new employees a "signing" bonus such as a cash payment or an agreement to cover the new employee's moving expenses.
- *Improve wages and fringe benefits.* Increasing wages will help increase the number of personnel willing to work in a particular position or occupation. However, employers are reluctant to do this because they may be forced to raise the wages of current employees as well. Further, unlike some other actions, once wages are raised, it is unlikely that they will be reduced later if hiring becomes less difficult.

- *Contract out the work.* If employers cannot fill vacancies for employees in certain occupations, they may contract out those tasks to another company.
- *Turn down work.* If an employer has exhausted other means to mitigate its hiring challenges and vacancies persist, it may choose to turn down work or curtail services.

Airlines and pilot schools have used a number of these strategies to attract more potential individuals to a career as an airline pilot. Economic literature suggests that increased recruiting is a logical first step to fill vacancies because it requires relatively fewer resources to implement than other potential options for attracting more interest in an occupation experiencing a shortage. Most of the airlines with whom we spoke reported that they have continued involvement with various recruiting activities, such as attending career events, including job fairs, and a couple of airlines reported that they had increased such activity to recruit more potential pilots. For example, representatives of one regional airline told us that after not hiring for several years and furloughing pilots, they have increased their recruiting efforts at some college aviation schools as well as Part 135 air service providers as part of their plan to begin hiring again. In addition, representatives from another airline said that they have almost doubled the size of their recruiting department to facilitate attendance at events and started to advertise new job openings— something they have not previously done.

Some collegiate pilot schools have also expanded recruiting efforts to the next generation of potential future pilots. Officials at some of the collegiate pilot schools we met with had developed outreach programs focused on local elementary and high school students to build interest in aviation, which economic literature suggests could limit any future labor shortages.[64] For example, Embry-Riddle Aeronautical University works with seven high schools that provide STEM-related courses (science, technology, engineering, and math) intended to immerse and prepare high school students in these academic areas for college as well as jobs in the aviation industry. In another example, the Metropolitan State University of Denver, which has a commercial pilot program, coordinates with other groups in Colorado to stimulate interest in careers in STEM fields from the preschool level through the graduate school level.

Airlines were also looking for ways to help new pilots to gain additional flight time and training to eventually qualify for an R-ATP or ATP certificate, and some regional and mainline airlines had begun to restructure "bridge agreements" with collegiate and vocational pilot schools.[65] Prior to the new pilot qualification rule, regional airlines would develop these arrangements with aviation schools as a way to directly recruit pilot graduates with a commercial pilot certificate and instrument rating as first officers, in which the airlines would typically lower their minimum hiring standards related to flight time and experience for desired pilots from these schools. Some regional and mainline airlines indicated that they had implemented such partnerships with pilot schools to promote greater interest in the field and provide a pathway from pilot school to employment as an airline pilot. For example, ExpressJet, a regional airline that contracts with Delta, has partnered with 11 collegiate aviation schools to offer selected students guaranteed employment at ExpressJet as a first officer and eventually a guaranteed interview at Delta Airlines once the student gains enough experience.

Since implementation of new pilot qualification rule requiring all airlines' first officers to have an ATP certificate, airlines have begun to change their bridge programs to help potential employees gain the necessary flight time and training to qualify for an ATP certificate. For example, two regional airlines are hiring pilots without an ATP certificate who are currently flight instructors. As airline employees, these pilots receive employee benefits such as medical and dental insurance, but continue instructing for a collegiate or vocational pilot school program to build flight time toward their ATP certification. Once these employees obtain an ATP certificate, they are placed into new hire classes to begin the airline's training program for first officers. Airlines and other stakeholders told us that they are also considering other options to adjust to the new pilot qualification rules, such as exploring new pathways to becoming an airline pilot and finding ways to improve pilot training, which will be discussed later in this report.

Regional airlines have started offering financial incentives to entice both graduating students and flight instructors. Offering financial incentives to new pilot hires is advantageous for airlines because it is a one-time cost and only affects the new employees hired. According to economic literature, signing bonuses are most frequently used when employers feel they are under intense pressure to fill vacancies in the short run. For example, two regional airlines that have had difficulty filling their new hire classes have started offering new-hire first officers an upfront $5,000 signing bonus, and one of these airlines also offers up to $10,000 for tuition reimbursement. However, officials of the industry association that represents these airlines told us that these efforts have essentially attracted pilot applicants away from other airlines, but they have not led to an increase in the applicant pool overall. DOD's Service branches have taken similar actions in direct response to addressing a potential shortage of military pilots by requiring longer service obligations and offering retention bonuses. For example, the U.S. Air Force recently began offering retention bonuses of up to $225,000 to its fighter jet pilots in exchange for a 9-year commitment.[66] This is an increase from the Air Force's previous retention offer of a 5-year contract for up to $25,000 per year, for a maximum of $125,000, in exchange for the commitment. Similarly, starting in fiscal year 2013, the U.S. Navy began offering retention bonuses to its pilots ranging from $25,000 to $125,000 for a 5- year commitment and paid over the term of the contract.

Economic literature also indicates that increasing wages is an obvious approach to increasing the number of workers willing to work in a particular occupation. However, 11 regional airlines with whom we spoke had not increased wages to attract better qualified applicants.[67] An increase in entry level pay for pilots at regional airlines could influence some pilots employed elsewhere (e.g., in the military, by foreign airlines, or in another industry) to consider seeking employment with these airlines. However, any increases in pay for pilots would be subject to negotiation of collective bargaining agreements between airlines and the pilot unions that represent the employed pilot workforce. As previously mentioned, raising wages is not a costless remedy. Since regional airlines generally provide service under capacity purchase agreements with mainline airlines on a contractual basis, regional airlines' ability to increase wages would likely be limited by their ability to increase revenue (i.e., increasing passenger fares).

Finally, economic literature indicates that contracting out or turning down work are options to cope with a labor shortage. Mainline airlines normally contract with regional airlines to expand available service. As previously mentioned, representatives of five regional airlines we interviewed told us that there have been some instances wherein the contracted capacity (i.e., scheduled flights) for mainline airline partners has had to be turned down by reducing and canceling flights due to a lack of pilot crew availability. According to an official of a small regional airline, for the first time in its history, the airline had to reduce about 20 percent of its scheduled flights in August 2013 because it could not staff all of its airplanes to provide the scheduled flights. Again, such actions are not costless and pose implications for the industry. A continued shortage of pilots for these airlines could mean additional curtailment of services, and thus far, it is smaller communities that are experiencing reduced service, and over a longer term may result in a contraction of the industry.

Federal Agencies Have a Limited Role in Helping to Attract People to Aviation-Related Careers

While no one agency is tasked with developing the pilot workforce, several maintain programs that help promote and train people for aviation-related careers. At the time of its creation in 1958, the FAA was tasked with regulating, promoting, encouraging, and developing civil aeronautics.[68] In 1996, following criticism of its response to the ValuJet crash in the Florida Everglades and to address concerns about its dual role, FAA's mission was amended to make ensuring the safety of the national air space system as the agency's top priority.[69] According to FAA, it has continued to promote careers in aviation, but specific references were deleted from its mandate. Nonetheless, FAA has several initiatives aimed at promoting the aviation industry and encouraging young people to pursue careers in aviation. For example, FAA developed the Aviation Career Education Academies, interactive aviation summer camps geared toward middle- and high-school students interested in aviation and aerospace; the agency also promotes DOT's National Transportation Summer Institute to introduce secondary school students to all modes of transportation careers and encourage them to pursue transportation-related courses of study at the postsecondary education level.[70] FAA also works with education and industry partners to offer initiatives such as adopt-a-school programs and other activities that expose students and others to aviation and aerospace. FAA works with industry, including the Experimental Aircraft Association, to facilitate the Young Eagle Program, which seeks to expose young people to aviation and give them an opportunity to fly in a general aviation airplane. In addition, FAA's Aviation and Space Education website is intended to appeal to an audience unfamiliar with aviation, such as students and teachers.

Other federal agencies provide financial assistance that is available for students that pursue aviation careers, including pilot training.

- DOD provides Military Tuition Assistance benefits to service members to help them enhance their professional development. The benefits can be used for pilot training or to pay for certification tests, such as an ATP certification.
- Education offers various federal aid benefits, such as low-interest student and parent loans, grants, and work-study funds to help cover educational expenses.[71] Collegiate aviation schools and some

vocational pilot schools are generally eligible to receive federal financial aid.

- VA administers education benefit programs, such as the Montgomery G.I. Bill, that can be used to pay for flight training for veterans who are interested in attending aviation programs approved by FAA, such as collegiate aviation schools and some vocational pilot schools.[72] The payment amount varies depending on the program and the type of pilot school. In addition, a 2011 law amended the Montgomery G.I. Bill program to provide financial assistance to veterans specifically for flight-training programs.[73]

- DOL administers programs under the Workforce Investment Act of 1998 (WIA) in which training services are available to eligible individuals who meet requirements for services—including training to become an airline pilot.[74] However, according to DOL, due to limited available resources, workforce counselors encourage individuals eligible for WIA training funds to also pursue educational funding from other sources (including VA and Education). Nevertheless, according to DOL data from 2010 through 2012, 124 individuals received WIA funding for pilot training.[75] In addition, apprenticeships are available for pilot occupations,[76] but there were no active apprentices as of November 2013.

- The Internal Revenue Code also provides tax credits—such as the American Opportunity Credit and Lifetime Learning Credit—and various deductions that may be taken to reduce the federal income tax burden for students or those paying the costs of students' post secondary education.[77]

Stakeholders Suggested Various Actions Government Could Take to Mitigate a Potential Shortage of Airline Pilots

Airline and pilot school stakeholders we interviewed suggested several actions that could be pursued by government to respond to potential shortages of airline pilots. These actions generally fell into two categories: (1) increasing the availability and flexibility of financial assistance available to aviation students and (2) creating additional pathways to becoming an airline pilot.

Increase Availability and Flexibility of Financial Assistance to Aviation Students

Several airline and pilot school officials we interviewed stated that the high cost of pilot training is deterring students from entering pilot school and pursuing an airline pilot career. To pay for pilot training, students typically use a mix of personal funds, personal credit (credit cards and personal loans), scholarships, grants, other private educational loans, and federal financial-assistance programs. However, flight school officials said that students enrolled in collegiate aviation schools and vocational pilot schools are finding it more difficult to qualify for financial aid because many private banks have been tightening restrictions on financing available to potential new-pilot students, and others have left the pilot training loan market. We previously found that in 2009, many lenders offering student loans had exited the market due to limited access to capital in response to the 2007-2009 financial crisis.[78] Since that time, according to officials of some pilot schools we interviewed, stricter lending standards continue to make it difficult for some students and parents to qualify for private loans.[79] In addition, unlike colleges and universities, many vocational pilot schools are not approved or accredited to offer federal financial-aid programs. Some of these schools offer financing options for those students who qualify by working with lenders including banks, credit unions, and private lending institutions. A number of stakeholders suggested that making it easier for all pilot schools to participate in federal student-loan programs could make it easier for schools to train more pilots because many students drop out due to financial difficulties.

Aviation stakeholders we interviewed in previous work agreed that one of most important challenges for maintaining an adequate supply of students for pilot schools is the availability of financial support. 80 Several airline and pilot school officials said the federal government could consider revising the existing student loan requirements for students in pilot schools seeking to become airline pilots—such as extending the loan repayment period, deferring the start of repaying the loan, and increasing the maximum loan amount—or establishing a student-loan repayment or forgiveness program for airline pilots. Loan forgiveness programs may include criteria for a specified length of employment and a required period of timely payments, upon which all or a portion of the remaining loan balance would be eliminated. Some stakeholders suggested that revising loan requirements could provide incentives to attract individuals to the pilot profession.

We have also previously found that European airlines have at times funded the training of pilot candidates in response to pilot shortages.[81] In the

European countries that we visited for our previous work, many student pilots, following a screening process, were provided training by airline sponsorship with an agreement for future employment with the airline. An example of an airline that follows this practice is Lufthansa, where students are offered the training as part of a partial sponsorship program, wherein candidates are required to pay a small portion of the training costs upfront while Lufthansa provides a student loan to students to cover this cost. Once training is completed, Lufthansa enters into an employment contract with the candidate, and he or she repays the loan by accepting a lower initial salary. Other European airlines have begun to assist their students by forming agreements with banks to reduce the risk of providing student loans to flight school students. British Airways helps students secure the funding required for training through a guaranteed bank loan in the hopes that this will increase the pool of qualified applicants. KLM partially funds an insurance policy to help banks cover their student loan default risks for students who end their pilot training early due to poor performance, failed medical examinations, or other unforeseen circumstances. If the insurance policy is executed, students are contractually obligated to cease their pursuit of an airline pilot career. None of the U.S. airlines we interviewed were currently considering such approaches.

Create Additional Pathways to Becoming an Airline Pilot

Some stakeholders suggested that FAA should consider supplementing the current regulatory framework for training new pilots with additional pathways to achieving an ATP certificate. Stakeholders have made these suggestions because the new pilot qualification rule changed the traditional pathway to becoming an airline pilot, and airlines initial experience under the new rule suggests that the flight hours new pilots are earning to qualify for an ATP certificate may not be directly relevant to an airline setting. Based on an exemption request to FAA from one of the member airlines, the Regional Air Cargo Carriers Association (RACCA) has supported a regulatory change that would allow first officers in Part 135 cargo-only operations to log certain flight hours that they are currently prohibited from logging, except under limited circumstances. According to RACCA officials, these first officers are frequently recent graduates of flight-training programs with commercial pilot certificates, and allowing the hours flown in these operations to count would give these pilots flight experience toward the qualifications for an ATP certificate that is more commensurate with flying for a passenger airline, since they are flying similar planes under similar conditions—unlike the flight hours logged in flight instruction using training airplanes, or through banner towing and similar types of flight experiences.[82] According to FAA officials, FAA is in the process of developing a proposed rulemaking that could expand the logging of flight time for certain Part 135 operations.

A proposal being developed by a consortium of industry stakeholders would request that FAA consider new regulations allowing the airline industry to take greater advantage of the advancements in computer-based and simulation technology for training pilots. According to the group, U.S. pilot training requirements for certification of airline pilots have not been significantly changed for decades and pilots have had to complete the same certification path based on the same training standards and requirements. While the standards for obtaining pilot certificates have changed little over the years, training technology has advanced through the use of simulation and computers. The group suggested that FAA should allow more credit for training using this type of technology in lieu of actual flying. The group argues that training aids provided by computer software, computer-based simulation, and flight simulation training can help students to achieve as good or better competency in various training components, such as aircraft performance, navigation, and aircraft systems operations. In fact, many of the collegiate aviation schools already provide specialized training in flight-simulation training devices, but FAA allows only a few of these training hours to be credited toward private and commercial pilot certificates. According to industry consortium, the ability to expand the use of these technologies would enable pilot schools to train the next generation of pilots more efficiently and improve the overall competency of entry-level first officers.

Many Asian and European countries have already adopted a similar approach in the form of the multi-crew pilot license (MPL)—an alternative pilot training and certification concept specifically geared toward training airline pilots.[83] The training methods for the MPL are focused on enhancing the quality of training geared toward first officer duties. Such competency-based training for pilots is not new and focuses on the training outcome in terms of how well students perform rather than simply meeting specified numbers of training hours.[84] Thus, training hours are replaced by sets of defined, measureable performance criteria. The MPL training model focuses on the core competencies that pilots need to be able to operate modern jet airplanes during all phases of flight. Many of the airline officials we interviewed suggested that this model for pilot training could serve as an additional career pathway for becoming a U.S. airline pilot.

CONCLUSION

Availability of a sufficient number of qualified pilots is vital to the U.S. airline industry and necessary to support air transportation services for passengers and cargo traveling within the United States or to and from this country. Evidence suggests that the supply pipeline is changing as fewer students enter and complete collegiate pilot-training programs and fewer military pilots are available than in the past. Additional pressure on pilot availability will come from (1) the projected number of mandatory age-related pilot retirements at mainline airlines over the next decade and beyond, (2) the increasing demand for regional airlines to address attrition needs, and (3) the reported lower number of potentially qualified pilots in the applicant pool for filling regional airlines' first-officer jobs. If the predictions for future demand are realized and shortages continue to develop, airlines may have to make considerable operational adjustments to compensate for having an insufficient number of pilots.

To address such a situation, opportunities exist for the airline industry to take action to attract more pilots. For example, airlines can continue to take actions that will promote aviation as an occupation—such as through employment pathway partnerships with pilot schools and additional career and financial support for pilots as they build flight hours for an R-ATP or ATP certificate. In addition, mainline and regional airlines could work together to shift some of the burden of increasing training costs from students as has been done by some European airlines and adjust contractual agreements between mainline and regional airline partners to help regional airlines increase revenue. Furthermore, with the mandate to increase pilot qualifications for airline pilots having only recently gone into effect, opportunities exist to develop new training methods and pathways for students to gain experience relevant to an airline environment. It is unclear at this point what adjustments could occur within the pilot training system that would help to respond to these stakeholders' concerns about the current regulations, or if government action may be necessary to enable certain changes. Therefore, we encourage FAA to continue its efforts in working with the airline and pilot training industries in considering additional ways for pilots to build quality flight time that contributes directly to working in airline operations. In the absence of efforts discussed in the report to incentivize and attract more people to the career, several airlines and industry stakeholders expressed some concern that service to some small communities may suffer going forward. Given the opportunities available for the industry to address a possible shortage of pilots, as discussed, as well as actions FAA is considering, we are not making recommendations in this report. In the event that Congress decides that actions in the market are not sufficient and it is necessary for government to intervene, this report offers several options for doing so.

AGENCY AND THIRD-PARTY COMMENTS

We provided a draft of this report to the departments of Defense, Labor, and Transportation for review and comment. DOD had no comments on the report. DOL and DOT provided technical comments that we incorporated as appropriate. In addition, to verify information, we sent relevant sections of the draft report to Airlines for America, the Regional Airlines Association, Malcolm Cohen, Ph.D., and various stakeholders, which also provided technical comments that we incorporated as appropriate.

Gerald L. Dillingham, Ph.D.
Director
Physical Infrastructure Issues

APPENDIX I: OBJECTIVES, SCOPE, AND METHODOLOGY

Our report focuses on the supply of and demand for airline pilots and potential market and government responses. In this report, we described (1) what the available data and forecasts reveal about the need for and potential availability of airline pilots and (2) the types of industry and government actions that are being taken, or might be taken, to attract and retain airline pilots.

To address the two objectives, we reviewed and synthesized a range of published reports from GAO, the Department of Transportation (DOT), and the Federal Aviation Administration (FAA) that included general background information on a variety of related issues, such as the pilot certification process; pilot training schools; typical career paths to become an airline pilot; piloting experience and airline pilot compensation; federal-funding programs for pilot training; and the historical and current health of the airline industry. We also reviewed relevant literature related to factors that affect the supply of and demand for airline pilots, including attrition and retention concerns, factors to consider in the future, and international pilot supply and demand issues based on search results from databases, such as ProQuest®, TRID, and Nexis®, as well as trade publications, industry stakeholder groups, and the Internet. Furthermore, we reviewed the federal aviation regulations related to training and certification for pilots under Parts 61 and 141, Title 14, Code of Federal Regulations (CFR); as well as oversight of air travel operations in accordance with Parts 91, 121, and 135, Title 14, CFR. We also reviewed provisions of the Airline Safety and Federal Aviation Administration Extension Act of 2010 (Pub. L. No. 111-216) related to "Flight Crewmember Screening and Qualifications" and "Airline Transport Pilot Certification." We reviewed FAA's regulatory final rules required by the Act related to addressing pilot fatigue (issued in January 2012);[1] increasing qualification requirements for first officers who fly U.S. passenger and cargo planes (issued in July 2013);[2] and enhancing pilot training requirements for airline pilots (issued in November 2013).[3]

To determine what the available data and forecasts reveal about the need for and potential availability of airline pilots, we reviewed relevant economic literature that describe labor market conditions[4]; developed a summary of the general economic principles for evaluating labor market conditions; and identified relevant data sources. Economic literature states that no single definition exists to define a labor shortage; however, one can look at multiple indicators—including unemployment rates, employment numbers, and earnings—which might converge to suggest either the presence or absence of a shortage.[5] We obtained these data from the Bureau of Labor Statistics (BLS) Current Population Survey (CPS) for years 2000 through 2012.[6] In 2010, the Standard Occupational Classification (SOC) system's occupation titles were updated and, as a result, some occupations' names were changed. We used SAS, a statistical software application, to connect the BLS CPS data for 2000-2010 and 2011-2012 by the SOC for aircraft pilots; this did not affect our occupation of interest.[7] We analyzed how these indicators have changed over time, and whether these indicators suggest a labor shortage—that is whether there appears to be an imbalance between the labor supply (i.e., available people) and demand (i.e., available jobs). We analyzed each occupation relative to all other occupations and using a scale with benchmarks developed in previous economic analysis.[8] For the unemployment rate we looked at the average unemployment rate for each occupation for 2000 through 2012.[9] For both employment and earnings we analyzed any change.[10] Due to the limitation that airline pilots and commercial pilots are combined into a single occupational category in the CPS data,[11] we also obtained data from the BLS

Occupational Employment Statistics (OES) survey for employment and wage earnings and analyzed any change from 2000 through 2012.[12] To verify our results, we consulted with Malcolm Cohen, Ph.D., labor economist and author of the original methodology for conducting indicator analysis.[13] We incorporated his comments as appropriate. Finally, we summarized limitations with the data with respect to how we used it. We determined the data were sufficiently reliable for the purposes of our indicator analysis to provide context on the labor market.

To identify future demand for, supply of, or employment, we analyzed projections for airline pilots in the United States. To identify relevant studies, we performed a literature review of scholarly material, government reports, and books, among others, to identify any employment projections for airline pilots and limited our results to those projecting employment in the United States (or North America) using databases that included ProQuest®, TRID, and Nexis®. We identified three demand-based forecasts—two conducted by government (FAA Aerospace Forecast Fiscal Years 2013-2033 and BLS Employment Projections 2012-2022), and one conducted by industry (Boeing Current Market Outlook 2013-2032)—and obtained each for analysis. To understand these projections, we reviewed the processes, methodologies, and sources of information used to make the projections. We also discussed the projections with knowledgeable staff involved with each study. We did not verify the data that the companies collected and used. Rather, we summarized the methodology and results for each and discussed any limitations we identified with respect to how the forecast was developed. We also described, based on economic literature, why forecasting generally includes a great deal of uncertainty.

We also identified and reviewed three relevant industry and academic studies that focused on the supply of and demand for airline pilots. The reviewed studies included (1) Lovelace, Higgins, et al, *An Investigation of the United States Airline Pilot Labor Supply,* 2013; (2) Brant Harrison from Audries Aircraft Analysis, *Pilot Demand Projections/Analysis for the Next 10 Years Full Model,* 2013; and (3) the MITRE Corporation, *Pilot Supply Outlook,* 2013. To evaluate these studies, we reviewed their methods, assumptions, and limitations. Each study was reviewed by one GAO economist, whose review was then verified by a second GAO economist. In our review of *An Investigation of the United States Airline Pilot Labor Supply*, we replicated the study's analysis using data provided by the lead researchers, which raised questions about a specific assumption made about future increases in the cost of pilot training. To determine the extent to which the conclusions of the study were based on this specific assumption, we varied the assumption to determine the extent to which that would lead to a different conclusion. We discussed our analysis in detail with the lead researchers, and in general, they acknowledged that our findings were valid, but provided reasons to explain why the original assumption used in the study was warranted.

To identify trends in supply sources for qualified airline pilots, we obtained data from 2000 through 2012 from civilian and military sources for pilots. We analyzed data from the Department of Education (Education) on annual completions by major in professional pilot programs; data from the Department of Defense (DOD) on expectations for the number of new pilots entering military service and separating from the military; and FAA's data on the number of individuals holding and obtaining pilot certificates and instrument ratings by year, specifically:

- *Education:* To describe national trends in completions in professional pilot degree programs, we analyzed data from Education's Integrated Postsecondary Education Data System (IPEDS). We used Education's Classification of Instructional Programs (CIP) and matched degree programs to our SOC codes to identify the relevant degree programs. Specifically, the CIP-SOC relationship indicates that programs classified in the CIP category prepare individuals directly for jobs classified in the SOC category. The categories of schools included in our analysis were degree granting: 4-year research, 4-year master, 4-year baccalaureate, 2-year associate, and vocational schools. Unless otherwise noted, data estimates for graduation rates are within a confidence interval of 5 percentage points.

- *DOD:* To better understand the role of the U.S. military as a source of potential airline pilots, we obtained data on military pilots separating from the Service branches (i.e., the Air Force, Army, Marine Corps, and Navy); the current number of pilots in each Service; and forecasted rates of separation for pilots. We interviewed military officials at the Pentagon to understand how separation trends in the future will compare to past trends.

- *FAA:* To better understand trends in the number of pilot certificates and instrument ratings held and new certificates issued, and age distribution of current airline transport pilot (ATP) certificate holders, we obtained data from FAA on pilot certificates and instrument ratings held and issued from 2000 through 2012. We also obtained data from FAA on the estimated number of active ATP certificates held by age group during this period in order to exclude the number of certificates held by pilots age 65 and older because they would not be allowed to work as airline pilots due to mandatory age retirement. The database in which certificate-holder information is stored maintains records on individuals until FAA is informed of their death.

To assess the reliability of Education, DOD, and FAA data, we reviewed documentation related to all data sources from prior GAO reports, the agencies' websites, and interviewed knowledgeable government officials about the quality of the data. We determined that the data were sufficiently reliable to describe general sources of supply of airline pilots and to support broad conclusions about trends in these sources over recent years.

To develop our list of actions that employers may take to mitigate labor shortages, we reviewed economic literature and interviewed the authors.[14] We also interviewed selected industry associations that represent airlines, the unions that represent pilots, and government officials to get a broader sense of the extent to which employers are taking actions to mitigate labor shortages. To supplement these broader trends, we also reviewed data from and interviewed representatives from passenger and cargo airlines, and selected collegiate aviation and non-collegiate vocational pilot schools. We contacted and gathered information from 10 mainline passenger and cargo airlines, and 12 regional passenger airlines.[15] We selected the mainline and regional airlines based on size in terms of passengers transported in 2012 and stakeholders' recommendations. While these 12 regional airlines are responsible for transporting about 71 percent of regional passengers in 2012, their views and experiences should not be used to make generalizations about all regional airlines. We also interviewed representatives of 10 collegiate aviation and 2 non-collegiate vocational pilot schools, which accounted for about half of the students who graduated with professional pilot majors in 2012. We selected these schools based on geographical diversity, average number of student enrollments in pilot training programs, stakeholders' recommendations, and our previous work related to pilot training. While these schools were among the largest schools in terms of student pilot enrollments, our findings should not be used to make generalizations about the views or experiences of all of the pilot training schools in the United States. We also met with and reviewed documents from various industry stakeholders, including pilot labor unions, airline associations, and industry organizations, among others (see table 2).

Table 2. Agencies, Organizations, and Airlines Contacted or Interviewed

U.S. federal agencies
Department of Education
Department of Defense
Department of Labor, Bureau of Labor Statistics
Department of Transportation, Federal Aviation Administration
Industry associations
Air Line Pilots Association
Airlines 4 America
Coalition of Airline Pilots Association
Independent Pilots Association
International Air Transport Association
National Business Aviation Association
Regional Airline Association
Regional Air Cargo Carriers Association
University Aviation Association
Industry organizations
Airline Apps, Inc.
Aviation Workforce Development
Boeing
CareerBuilder
Families of Continental Flight 3407
International Civil Aviation Organization
Venture Management, Inc
Collegiate aviation pilot schools
Embry-Riddle Aeronautical University, Daytona Beach, Florida
Embry-Riddle Aeronautical University, Prescott, Arizona
Kansas State University at Salina
Metropolitan State University
Middle Tennessee State University
Purdue University
Southern Illinois University
Tarrant County College
University of North Dakota
Western Michigan University
Non-collegiate vocational pilot schools
Aerosim Flight Academy
FlightSafety Academy

Table 2. (Continued)

Mainline airlines
Alaska Airlines
American Airlines
Atlas Air
Delta Airlines
Hawaiian Airlines
JetBlue Airways
Southwest Airlines
United Airlines
United Parcel Service
US Airways
Regional airlines
American Eagle Airlines
ExpressJet
Great Lakes Airlines
Mesa Air
Republic Airways Holdings (Chautauqua Airlines, Republic Airlines, Shuttle America)
Silver Airways
SkyWest Airlines
Trans States Holdings, Inc. (Trans States Airlines, Compass Airlines, GoJet Airlines)

Source: GAO.

We conducted this performance audit from March 2013 through February 2014 in accordance with generally accepted government auditing standards. Those standards require that we plan and perform the audit to obtain sufficient, appropriate evidence to provide a reasonable basis for our findings and conclusions based on our audit objectives. We believe that the evidence obtained provides a reasonable basis for our findings and conclusions based on our audit objectives.

End Notes

[1] Data on pilots employed were retrieved from the Bureau of Transportation Statistics' TranStats Web site.

[2] GAO recently performed similar work focused on the supply of and demand for aviation professionals—including aerospace engineers, aircraft mechanics, and avionics technicians—see GAO, *Aviation Workforce: Information on Current and Future Availability of Aviation Professionals*, GAO-14-237 (Washington, D.C.: February 2014).

[3] See Malcolm S. Cohen, *Labor Shortages as America Approaches the Twenty-first Century* (Ann Arbor, The University of Michigan Press: 1995); James Bell Associates for Department of Labor, *Labor Shortages Case Studies*, (Arlington, VA: 1993); and Carolyn M. Veneri, "Can Occupational Labor Shortages Be Identified Using Available Data?" *Monthly Labor Review* (March 1999).

[4] We used the SOC detailed occupation 53-2011 for "Airline Pilots, Copilots, and Flight Engineers." This number does not include individuals in the SOC detailed occupation 53-2012 for "Commercial Pilots" who are not employed by airlines. The SOC system is used by federal statistical agencies to classify workers into occupational categories for the purpose of collecting, calculating, or disseminating data.

[5] Mainline airlines provide domestic and international passenger and cargo service on larger aircraft. Regional airlines provide domestic and limited international passenger service, generally using aircraft with fewer than 90 seats, and cargo service to smaller airports.

[6] 14 C.F.R. Part 121 prescribes rules governing the domestic, flag, and supplemental operations to hold an air carrier certificate. Scheduled-service airlines are generally issued a Part 121 certificate by FAA and operate turbojet-powered airplanes or airplanes with more than nine passenger seats or airplanes having a payload capacity of more than 7,500 pounds.

[7] Under a capacity purchase agreement, mainline airlines contract with regional airlines to provide air service beyond the mainline airline's route network to increase their capacity and revenue. Agreement terms vary, but mainline airlines generally take on all commercial functions, such as brand marketing, flight scheduling, and ticket pricing while the regional airlines are responsible for the aircraft and crews to operate the flights, and provide ground and flight operations.

[8] 14 C.F.R. Part 135 prescribes rules governing the commuter or on-demand operations to hold an air carrier certificate. Nonscheduled-service airlines are generally issued a Part 135 certificate by FAA and operate aircraft other than turbojet-powered airplanes having no more than nine passenger seats and a payload capacity of 7,500 pounds or less.

[9] 14 C.F.R. Part 61 prescribes the minimum training, knowledge, and experience requirements for acquiring a pilot certificate.

[10] A rating defines the conditions or type of aircraft in which a pilot certificate may be used. In addition, endorsements by flight instructors may be given to pilots to further define conditions or specific aircraft not covered by ratings.

[11] The University Aviation Association is the representative voice of college aviation education to the aviation industry, government agencies, and the general public.

[12] In commercial aviation, the pilot-in-command (captain) of an aircraft is the person aboard the aircraft who is ultimately responsible for its operation and safety during all phases of flight, as well as when it is operating or moving on the ground, in accordance with FAA's regulations. The second-in-command (first officer) is the second pilot of an aircraft, and has the authority to assume command of the aircraft in the event of incapacitation of the captain. However, control of the aircraft is normally shared equally between the captain and first officer during flight.

[13] Pub. L. No. 111-216, 124 Stat. 2348 (2010).

[14] 77 Fed. Reg. 330 (Jan. 4, 2012).

[15] 78 Fed. Reg. 42324 (July 15, 2013). The Airline Safety and Federal Aviation Administration Extension Act of 2010 also stated that in the event that FAA failed to meet the deadline for conducting the necessary rulemaking to implement a new requirement for all airline pilots to have an ATP certificate, the requirement would begin to automatically apply 3 years after the date of enactment of the law, or approximately August 2, 2013. Pub. L. No. 111-216, § 216 (c), 124 Stat. 2348, 2367 (2010).

[16] As required by law, in order to enhance the academic training and operational experience requirements for airline pilots, FAA created the ATP Certification Training Program (ATP CTP) to be a prerequisite for pilots to take the knowledge test to obtain an ATP certificate—to be effective August 1, 2014. Pub. L. No. 111-216, § 217, 124 Stat. 2348, 2367. The program includes training in aerodynamics, automation, adverse weather conditions, air carrier operations, transport airplane performance, leadership, and professional development. Also, the program requires that pilots receive 10 hours of training in flight simulation training devices: 6 hours in a Level C or higher full-motion flight simulator, and 4 hours in Level 4 or higher flight training simulation device. Further, to serve to as a first officer for an airline, a pilot with an ATP or R-ATP certificate must also obtain an appropriate type rating for the aircraft for which he or she operates for the airline. FAA's new pilot qualification rule, in response to concerns about the lack of sufficient number of training devices to deliver the ATP CTP, stated there were currently 407 FAA-evaluated Level C or higher full-motion flight simulator devices that replicate aircraft with a maximum takeoff weight at or exceeding 40,000 pounds. These devices represent 98 percent of all Level C and D full-motion flight simulators that have been approved by the FAA. Also, there were 81 Level 4 or higher flight training simulation devices. Based on FAA's analysis of usage for these devices, FAA determined there was sufficient inventory of these devices available to accommodate the requirements of the ATP CTP training course, even with the moderate usage for training unrelated to the course.

[17] Section 217(d).

[18] 14C.F.R. § 61.160(a), (b), and (c), respectively. An ATP certificate requires that a pilot be 23 years of age (14 CFR 61.153(a)(1)), have 1,500 hours total time as a pilot and 500 hours of cross-country flight time (14 CFR 61.159(a)). To qualify for an R-ATP, a pilot must be 21 years of age (14 CFR 61.153(a)(2)) and have 200 hours of cross-country flight time (14 CFR 61.160(f)). The 200 hours of cross-country experience represents a significant increase over the 50 hours of cross-country flight time required for the commercial pilot certificate—the prior requirement to serve as a first officer in part 121 operations. Pilots who hold an R–ATP certificate will be required to meet the 500 hours of cross-country flight time required in section 61.159 prior to having the limitation removed from their certificate. The rule also included a regulatory provision that allows a pilot who is at least 21 years old, and has 1,500 hours of total time as a pilot and 200 hours of cross-country flight time to be eligible for an R-ATP.

[19] In order to qualify for the R-ATP with a minimum of 1,000 hours of total time as a pilot, the graduating pilot must hold a bachelor's degree with an aviation major from an institution of higher education and complete 60 semester credit hours of aviation and aviation-related coursework that has been recognized by the FAA Administrator as coursework designed to improve and enhance the knowledge and skills of a person seeking a career as a professional pilot. 14 CFR 61.160(b).

[20] In order to qualify for the R-ATP with a minimum of 1,250 hours of total time as a pilot, the graduating pilot must hold a bachelor's or an associate's degree with an aviation major and complete 30 aviation semester credit hours, who also receives a commercial pilot certificate

and instrument rating, from an institution of higher education that has been recognized by the FAA Administrator as coursework designed to improve and enhance the knowledge and skills of a person seeking a career as a professional pilot. 14 CFR 61.160(c).

[21] Instrument rating is the qualification that allows a pilot to operate an aircraft under the rules and procedures for flying solely by reference to an aircraft's instruments (Instrument Flight Rules) instead of by visual reference (Visual Flight Rules). While an instrument rating requires additional training and instruction beyond what is required for a private pilot or commercial pilot certificate, it is not issued at a certain pilot certification level and is merely an operating privilege.

[22] This estimate assumes a total of 4 years to complete a collegiate aviation degree program, obtaining a commercial pilot certificate and instrument rating, and 1-2 years spent gaining the additional experience and number of flight hours to qualify for an ATP certificate.

[23] The holder of a valid flight instructor certificate may provide pilot training and instruction for pilot certification in any aircraft for which they are qualified. 14 C.F.R. § 61.183.

[24] 14 C.F.R. Part 91 outlines the federal aviation regulations for the basic rules governing all flight operations. Pilots with commercial pilot certificates can be hired to operate aircraft under Part 91 for government operations (e.g., law enforcement, agricultural, environmental, and emergency response), banner towing, sightseeing operations, pipeline patrol, and corporate flights.

[25] Part 61 allows for a maximum of 25 hours of training in a full flight simulator representing a multiengine airplane to be credited toward the flight time requirement for an ATP certificate if the training was accomplished as part of a FAA-approved training course. 14 C.F.R. § 61.159(a)(3). In addition, no more than 100 hours of the total non-airplane time towards the total time requirement for an ATP certificate which may be obtained in a full flight simulator or flight training device provided the device represents an airplane and the aeronautical experience was accomplished as part of a FAA-approved training course. 14 C.F.R. § 61.159(a)(5).

[26] A labor shortage is similar in definition to a "skills gap." GAO recently reported that officials from BLS indicated the following conditions would be associated with a skills gap in a particular occupation: 1) jobs remain unfilled for a longer-than-normal time period, 2) wages are increasing, and 3) unemployment is low. GAO, *Workforce Investment Act: Local Areas Face Challenges Helping Employers Fill Some Types of Skilled Jobs*, GAO-14-19 (Washington, D.C.: December 2013).

[27] A labor shortage occurs when demand for workers for a particular occupation is greater than the number ("supply") of workers who are qualified, available, and willing to do the work at a current wage rate.

[28] All data on the unemployment rate, employment, and earnings come from BLS's CPS unless otherwise noted.

[29] Cohen, *Labor Shortages*. In Cohen's analysis, growth rates are calculated by computing the year over year change or annualizing the data; the resulting year-over-year change is then located on a scale from 1 to 7 developed by Cohen, where 1 corresponds to strong indication of a labor surplus and 7 corresponds to strong indication of a labor shortage. Rather than looking at annualized data, we calculated the change in average annual growth, since calculating the data this way allowed us to calculate the significance of any trends. Although this resulted in larger year-to-year changes, it did not affect our interpretation of any of the results.

[30] Cohen, *Labor Shortages*.

[31] The SOC for airline pilots includes those who pilot and navigate the flight of fixed-wing, multi-engine aircraft, usually on scheduled airline routes, for the transport of passengers and cargo, and commercial pilots are those involved in other flight activities, such as piloting helicopters, crop dusting, charter flights, and aerial photography. The BLS CPS data for unemployment, wage earnings, and employment combined both occupational categories, but the BLS OES survey subdivides its employment and earnings data for airline pilots and commercial pilots.

[32] For the economy overall, since 2000, the average unemployment rate has been 6.3 percent, median earnings have not increased, and employment has stayed about the same.

[33] By changing the base year to 2001, for example, we would have estimated a different percentage change because the period was different. To ensure that these growth rates were not driven by our decision of the baseline year, we also estimated the average year-to-year growth by linear regression, and found similar results for annual growth rates of - 0.37 percent per year. However, the decline was not statistically significant.

[34] As stated previously, a limitation of the CPS data is that both airline and commercial pilots are combined into a single occupational category. For wages, data from an alternate source, the OES survey found that airline pilots median annual wages fell by 23 percent from 2000 to 2012, after correcting for inflation, whereas commercial pilots' median wages increased by 27 percent.

[35] As stated previously, a limitation of the CPS data is that both airline and commercial pilots are combined into a single occupational category.

[36] A type rating permits pilots to operate specific kinds of aircraft and can be obtained with the various types of pilot certificates. A type rating involves additional training and testing that is specific to the airplane for which the rating is being sought to enable a pilot to operate.

[37] BLS conducts a Job Openings and Labor Turnover Survey that provides a broad measure of job vacancies, but not by occupation.

[38] Carolyn M. Veneri, "Can Occupational Labor Shortages be Identified Using Available Data?" *Monthly Labor Review* (March 1999) 15-21.

[39] See Audries Aircraft Analysis, *Pilot Demand Projections/Analysis for the Next 10 Years: Full Model* (2013).

[40] See Lovelace, Higgins, et al, *An Investigation of the United States Airline Pilot Labor Supply* (University of North Dakota, 2013). In 2012, various stakeholders within the aviation industry formed a group to analyze the current state of the pilot labor supply for U.S. airlines. Within this stakeholders group, a subgroup of collegiate aviation researchers formed to provide the scientific research related to this topic, and included researchers from the University of Nebraska Omaha; Embry-Riddle Aeronautical University; Southern Illinois University; LeTourneau University; and Middle Tennessee State University.

[41] The BLS projections relied on a basic assumption of an economy with full employment in the projected year.

[42] The Airline Monitor is a commercially available aircraft forecast used by financial companies and other businesses who rely upon forecast information for strategic planning purposes.

[43] FAA, *FAA Aerospace Forecast Fiscal Years 2013-2033* (2013).

[44] FAA, *Final Regulatory Evaluation Pilot Certification and Qualification Requirements for Air Carrier Operations Office of Aviation Policy and Plans*, Economic Analysis Division (APO-300) (June 2013). FAA's projection started with 78,728 pilots being employed by airlines at the end of 2011. FAA then projected that the number of airline pilots is estimated to grow at a forecast rate of 0.6 percent each year. The number of retiring pilots was calculated by multiplying the number of pilots in the previous year by an estimated

retirement rate of 3.6 percent. The number of new pilots was calculated as the annual change in the number of pilots plus the change in the number of retiring pilots to account for replacement pilots.

[45] An active pilot is a person with a pilot certificate and a valid medical certificate. Pilots are required to obtain a medical certificate that indicates they have passed a physical exam by a FAA-authorized doctor. 14 CFR 61.23. To remain current for most types of pilot certificates, pilots must undergo a medical examination at various intervals. While airline captains must hold first-class medical certificates—requiring the most extensive medical examination—which must be renewed every 12 months for pilots under age 40 and every six months for pilots age 40 and over, first officers are allowed to hold second-class medical certificates which must be renewed every 12 months for all pilots regardless of age. 14 CFR 61.23(d). FAA data show a total of 109,465 currently active pilots under age 65 with a first class medical certificate holding ATP certificates, as of January 30, 2014. We excluded the number of certificates held by pilots age 65 and older because they would not be allowed to work as airline pilots due to mandatory age retirement.

[46] FAA forecasts future ATP certificate holders based on historical trends in pilots with instrument rating and the number of aircraft in the commercial jet fleet.

[47] While commercial and ATP certificate pools have remained steady, the number of pilots under age 65 holding private pilot certificates decreased 24 percent from 2000 through 2012, while the number of new certificates issued was 39 percent lower in 2012 than 2000 (16,571 compared to 27,223).

[48] Data from 1990 through 2012 was gathered from Future and Active Pilot Advisors (FAPA.aero), a career and financial advisory service for pilots and aspirants, for the historical hiring of pilots at major airlines.

[49] The Education data contains a small number of non-collegiate vocational schools that do not participate in federal student aid programs. It is possible that a small number of these schools are captured in our analysis if they offer pilot training programs related to the airline pilot occupation for which we collected data.

[50] Data on enrollments in pilot education programs nationally are not available.

[51] Flight instructors' pay is generally based on the number of hours that can be billed for providing instruction and whether they are employed part time or full time. According to FAA, full-time flight instructors can, in many instances, make more than a regional airline first officer, depending on demand for pilot instruction in a local area.

[52] DOD provided data for the U.S. Air Force, U.S. Army, U.S. Navy, and Marine Corps.

[53] Brant Harrison from Audries Aircraft Analysis, *Pilot Demand Projections/Analysis for the Next 10 Years Full Model*, 2013; and the MITRE Corporation, *Pilot Supply Outlook* (2013).

[54] MITRE Corporation, *Pilot Supply Outlook* (2013).

[55] Lovelace, Higgins, et al, *An Investigation of the United States Airline Pilot Labor Supply.*

[56] As discussed earlier, this forecast is on the higher end of existing pilot employment projections, such as those from FAA, BLS, and aircraft manufacturers.

[57] This is especially true if the nature of the economic series does not necessarily imply a trend, such as inflation, which measures the change in price and not price itself. For example, over the past 50 years, U.S. inflation has been as high as 14 percent and as low as -0.3 percent, but does not appear to have followed any 20-year trends.

[58] Regional airlines hire first officers with varying numbers of flight hours, depending on the preferred minimum qualifications of the airline, its need, and the available supply of pilots at the point in time the hiring is occurring. Previous to the new rule, the total hours accrued by a new-hire first officer could be higher or lower than the range of 500 to 700 hours

mentioned here. Data on the average number of hours of new hires across all regional airlines for the years prior to the new rule are not available. However, a Regional Airline Association's review of its members in 2009 found an average of 1,305 flight hours for new hires across the responding regional airlines.

[59] An airline pilot's annual salary is calculated by the hourly rate times the "minimum guarantee" number of hours flown each month that each airline sets in its pilots' contract. The minimum guarantee is generally about 75 hours per month but varies by airline. Pilots may fly less than the guarantee but are still paid for the minimum guarantee hours. If they fly more flight hours than the minimum guarantee, then they will get paid for the additional time flown.

[60] According to a 2010 FAA survey of industry, in terms of the career path of a typical airline pilot, the average number of years for a regional airline first officer to upgrade to a regional airline captain is about 5 years for airlines that use regional jets and/or turboprop airplanes; after 2 years as regional airline captain, the pilot moves to a position as mainline airline first officer; and after an additional 10 years, the pilot upgrades to mainline airline captain.

[61] Operating under Part 135 rules would allow an airline to operate multiengine airplanes with a first officer who has a commercial pilot certificate and an instrument rating.

[62] Burt S. Barnow, John Trutko, and Jaclyn Piatak, "Conceptual Basis for Identifying and Measuring Occupational Labor Shortages." In *Occupational Labor Shortages: Concepts, Causes, Consequences, and Cures* (Kalamazoo, MI: W.E. Upjohn Institute for Employment Research, 2013) 1-34.

[63] Such actions mentioned in the literature include (1) *increasing the use of overtime*, which is not a feasible strategy for airlines, since regulation limits the number of duty hours for pilots; (2) *restructuring the work to use current or new employees in other occupations*, which is not a feasible option for airlines to consider since FAA regulates minimum qualifications for becoming a pilot as well as minimum requirements for operating aircraft; and (3) *substituting machinery and equipment for labor*, which would be analogous to increasing automation in airplanes so fewer pilots would be needed; however, airlines cannot arbitrarily make these determinations, as FAA regulates minimum pilot requirements for operating aircraft and would have to approve the use of any new onboard equipment.

[64] Cohen, *Labor Shortages*.

[65] A "bridge agreement" can be a formal agreement through signed documentation or an informal arrangement between a regional airline and an aviation pilot school. Typical conditions of the agreement stipulate a specific grade point average, minimum number of flight hours, and other desirable academic qualifications for the students.

[66] Eligible pilots have the option to take an upfront lump sum payout of half of the money, minus taxes, with the remainder paid over the nine years of the contract. Also, Air Force pilots earn about $90,000 in base pay by their 11th year in service.

[67] However, one small regional airline we interviewed recently announced an agreement with the unions that represent their pilots to increase pilot pay, but final approval is subject to ratification by the airline's pilot membership. If ratified by the pilots, the agreement will immediately increase pay and commuting and schedule flexibility, and allow all pilots who remain with the airline for a year to earn a cash retention bonus.

[68] Pub. L. No. 85-726, § 103(a) and (b), 305, 72 Stat. 731, 740 and 749 (1958).

[69] On May 11, 1996, a ValuJet DC-9 crashed into the Florida Everglades shortly after takeoff from Miami International Airport, killing all 110 people aboard. Earlier that year, FAA had initiated a special review of the rapidly-growing low-cost carrier following a series of incidents and non-fatal accidents. In June 1996, FAA announced that the carrier would

cease operations pending safety improvements to address serious deficiencies it had found in ValuJet's airworthiness, maintenance, quality oversight, and engineering capabilities. This sparked renewed criticism of DOT and FAA because it appeared to contrast with statements, made following the accident, assuring the public that the airline was safe. The next day, Secretary of Transportation committed to urge Congress to make safety FAA's single primary mission. The change was codified in the Federal Aviation Reauthorization Act of 1996, Pub. L. No. 104-264, § 401, 110 Stat. 3213, 3255 (1996).

[70] FAA collaborated with the Federal Highway Administration to combine the two youth summer programs to increase education outreach from pre-kindergarten to institutions of higher education.

[71] The Department of Education's Office of Federal Student Aid manages and administers student financial-assistance programs authorized under Title IV of the Higher Education Act of 1965, as amended, (codified at 20 U.S.C. §§ 1070 – 1099d and 42 U.S.C. §§ 2571 – 2756b), which include student loans, grants, and campus-based work study aid.

[72] VA benefits can only be used for flight training provided by FAA-approved Part 141 pilot schools, but not by flight-training providers that operate under Part 61— often provided by an individual, for-hire flight instructor who can operate independently as a single-instructor school at a local airport. Also, VA benefits can be used for flight training if the veteran holds a private pilot certificate upon beginning the training and meets the medical requirements.

[73] The Post-9/11 Veterans Educational Assistance Improvements Act of 2010 authorizes payment of the actual net costs for in-state tuition and fees assessed by the school or $10,000, whichever is less, per academic year. Pub. L. No. 111-377, § 105(b), 124 Stat. 4106, 4113 (2011).

[74] Pub. L. No. 105-220, 112 Stat. 936 (1998).

[75] The number of individuals who received WIA funding for pilot training represent a small percentage of the total number of WIA funding recipients.

[76] Under the apprenticeship program, individuals earn a salary while receiving work-based training.

[77] Tax credits directly reduce the amount of income tax owed, while deductions reduce the amount of taxable income upon which income taxes are computed. The American Opportunity Credit applies to the first 4 years of post-secondary education up to $2,500 of the cost of qualified tuition and related expenses paid during the taxable year. The Lifetime Learning Credit has no limit on the number of years the credit can be claimed for each student and applies up to $2,000 for all levels of post-secondary education coursework. American Recovery and Reinvestment Tax Act, Pub. L. No. 111-5, §1004, 123 Stat. 306, 314.

[78] GAO, *Initial Pilot Training: Better Management Controls Are Needed to Improve FAA Oversight*, GAO-12-117, (Washington, D.C.: November 2011) and GAO, *Higher Education: Factors Lenders Consider in Making Lending Decisions for Private Education Loans*, GAO-10-86R (Washington, D.C.: November 2009).

[79] Traditionally, most student loans were available through two programs: the William D. Ford Federal Direct Loan Program (Direct Loan), in which the federal government provides loans directly to students through their schools, and the Federal Family Education Loan Program (FFEL), in which private lenders provide loans guaranteed by the federal government. However, the Student Aid and Fiscal Responsibility Act, enacted as part of the Health Care and Education Reconciliation Act of 2010, terminated the authority to make or insure new FFEL loans after June 30, 2010, so that most federal loans are now originated

under the Direct Loan Program. Pub. L. No. 111-152, § 2201, 124 Stat. 1029, 1074 (2010). While private lenders no longer provide federally guaranteed student loans, they may continue to provide private loans which are not federally subsidized. As a result, lenders may use other criteria to determine borrower eligibility and loan interest rates.

[80] GAO-12-117.

[81] GAO-12-117.

[82] RACCA also supports another member airline's petition to FAA for an exemption to reduce the requirement of 1,200 hours of total time to 800 hours for captains in Part 135 cargo-only operations under Instrument Flight Rules, which, if allowed, would only be applicable to all cargo flying in less advanced, non-type-rated airplanes (i.e., below 12,500 lb. maximum takeoff weight and not turbojet-powered). A RACCA official stated this would provide another option to increase experience and qualification in larger airplanes and help the pilot supply pipeline for the U.S. airline industry.

[83] In November 2006, the International Civil Aviation Organization (ICAO) enabled the implementation for the multi-crew pilot license by amending personnel licensing standards to include a new pilot certificate and adopting new standards for this *ab initio* airline pilot training method. ICAO is the international body that, among other things, promulgates international standards and recommended practices in an effort to harmonize global aviation standards.

[84] The international standards for an approved MPL training program specify a minimum of 240 hours of actual and simulated training, but do not specify a descriptive breakdown of hours for the program.

End Notes for Appendix I

[1] 77 Fed. Reg. 330 (Jan. 4, 2012).

[2] 78 Fed. Reg. 42324 (July 15, 2013).

[3] 78 Fed. Reg. 67800 (Nov. 12, 2013).

[4] Barnow, Trutko, and Piatak, *Conceptual Basis for Identifying and Measuring Occupational Labor Shortages*, and Cohen, *Labor Shortages*.

[5] In the absence of a universally agreed upon definition, we have defined a labor shortage in the same terms that have been used in economic literature, including a BLS publication.

[6] The Current Population Survey, a monthly household survey conducted by the Bureau of the Census for the BLS, provides a comprehensive body of information on the employment and unemployment experience of the nation's population, classified by age, sex, race, and a variety of other characteristics.

[7] Occupation titles were updated in 2010 and some occupations were combined and others were phased out. While this did not affect our occupations, it affected the total number of occupations. We excluded those occupation for which the name changed. We also excluded occupations that had any years where the sample size was too small (i.e., under 50,000 observations) to report unemployment, median weekly earnings, or employment. This affected unemployment and weekly earnings more than employment. As a result, we dropped 288, 490, and 250 occupations from the unemployment rate, employment, and earnings, respectively.

[8] Cohen developed a scale with seven categories to more easily synthesize results from the indictors. Each occupation's indicators were assigned a numerical value from 1 to 7.

Categories were developed by looking at the distribution of the results and setting natural groupings (e.g., distinguishing between positive and negative employment growth). A rank of "7" designates the indicator is consistent with a labor shortage and a "1" designates the indicator is consistent with a labor surplus.

[9] As part of a sensitivity analysis we also compared data since 2003, in addition to developing a regression line for both time periods. Performing multiple analyses with different comparison years allowed us to ensure that a year with unique results would not impact our analysis.

[10] Similar to the unemployment rate we also looked at data since 2003 as well. Finally, we adjusted earnings for inflation and only included full-time non-farm workers.

[11] BLS defines airline pilots as those who work for airline companies that transport passengers and cargo according to fixed schedules, and commercial pilots are those involved in other flight activities, such as crop dusting, charter flights, and aerial photography. BLS's Current Population Survey data for unemployment, wage earnings, and employment combined both occupational categories.

[12] The Occupational Employment Statistics (OES) program produces employment and wage estimates annually for over 800 occupations for the nation as a whole, individual States, metropolitan and nonmetropolitan areas, and national occupational estimates for specific industries. BLS subdivides its employment and earnings data for airline pilots and commercial pilots.

[13] Dr. Malcolm S. Cohen, President of Employment Research Corporation, received his Ph.D. in Economics from the Massachusetts Institute of Technology in 1967. Dr. Cohen has directed numerous labor market research and forecasting studies for the U.S. Department of Labor. Dr. Cohen testifies as an expert witness in various court proceedings on economic loss, discrimination, and other employment issues.

[14] Barnow, Trutko, and Piatak, *Conceptual Basis for Identifying and Measuring Occupational Labor Shortages.*

[15] Mainline airlines provide domestic and international passenger and cargo service on larger aircraft. Regional airlines provide domestic and limited international passenger service, generally using aircraft with fewer than 90 seats, and cargo service to smaller airports.

In: Airline Pilots and Aviation Professionals   ISBN: 978-1-63321-035-6
Editor: Angela Dillinger   © 2014 Nova Science Publishers, Inc.

Chapter 2

AVIATION WORKFORCE: CURRENT AND FUTURE AVAILABILITY OF AVIATION ENGINEERING AND MAINTENANCE PROFESSIONALS[*]

United States Government Accountability Office

WHY GAO DID THIS STUDY

Maintaining a safe and robust aviation system requires qualified aviation professionals—including aerospace engineers, aircraft mechanics, and avionics technicians—to design, manufacture, and repair more than 225,000 aircraft. Aviation stakeholders have expressed concerns that an insufficient supply of personnel could develop because of imminent retirements and a perception that fewer people enter these professions.

GAO was asked to review the supply and demand of aviation professionals. This report discusses (1) what available data and forecasts reveal about the need for and potential availability of aerospace engineers, aircraft mechanics, and avionics technicians, and (2) what actions industry and the federal government are taking to help attract and retain these professionals. GAO (1) collected and analyzed data from 2000 through 2012, employment projections from 2012 through 2022, and literature relevant to the aviation

---

[*] This is an edited, reformatted and augmented version of United States Government Accountability Office Publication, No. GAO-14-237, dated February 2014.

professionals' labor markets; (2) reviewed agency documents; and (3) interviewed agency officials about programs that support training. GAO also interviewed 10 aviation industry associations (5 representing employees and 5 representing employers) and selected a non-generalizable sample of 23 private sector employers, based on size and location, to understand any actions used to attract their workforce.

GAO is not making recommendations. GAO received technical comments on this report from Education, DOL, and DOT, which were incorporated as appropriate. DOD did not have any comments on this report.

WHAT GAO FOUND

GAO analysis found mixed evidence about a current or possible future shortage of aviation professionals. Aerospace engineers have experienced a low unemployment rate—the most direct measure of a labor shortage—and increases in employment suggesting a shortage may exist; however, earnings for the occupation have stayed about the same. Data provide less support for a shortage of aircraft mechanics; while the occupation has had a low unemployment rate, both employment and earnings have stayed about the same, suggesting that demand for this occupation has not outstripped supply. GAO was unable to analyze information on avionics technicians because of insufficient data. In addition, the Bureau of Labor Statistics' employment projections indicate slower than average or no growth for these three occupations over the next 10 years. Data also suggest the number of people who have received training related to these aviation professions is increasing; however, several other industries compete for these individuals and not all will pursue aviation careers.

Industry and government are taking some actions to attract and retain qualified individuals in these occupations, but employers GAO interviewed remain concerned about future needs. GAO found that most of these employers had some challenges hiring personnel with the skills employers were seeking at the wage they offered. According to economic literature, employers may take several actions in response to a perceived labor shortage—including increasing recruiting efforts and raising wages. Employers reported taking a variety of actions, but few were raising wages. Several agencies—the Federal Aviation Administration (FAA) and the Departments of Defense (DOD), Education, Labor (DOL), and Veterans Affairs—maintain programs that assist individuals interested in aviation careers. For example, in academic year 2011–2012, Education disbursed approximately $1.6 billion in federal grants to students majoring in related fields. Still, most employers and stakeholders stated that maintaining a qualified workforce will be difficult, in part because of a perception that fewer people are interested in aviation careers. GAO was unable to verify these concerns with available data. It could be expected that employers would continue to take actions at their disposal—such as adjusting wages or changing recruiting and training practices—if a labor shortage were to develop. While such actions would be considered typical market responses to a potential shortage, it does not mean such actions are costless or might not affect the industry.

ABBREVIATIONS

A&P	airframe and power plant
AMT	aviation maintenance technician
AVSED	Office of Aviation and Space Education
BLS	Bureau of Labor Statistics
Boeing	Boeing Company
CIP	Classification of Instructional Programs
CPS	Current Population Survey
DOD	Department of Defense
DOL	Department of Labor
DOT	Department of Transportation
Education	Department of Education
FAA	Federal Aviation Administration
ICAO	International Civil Aviation Organization
IPEDS	Integrated Postsecondary Education Data System
JSAMTCC	Joint Services Aviation Maintenance Technician Certification Council
Manufacturer	original equipment manufacturer
NASCAR	National Association for Stock Car Auto Racing, Inc.
NDAA	National Defense Authorization Act
NPSAS	National Postsecondary Student Aid Study
Repair Station	maintenance, repair, and overhaul facility
STEM	science, technology, engineering, and math
SOC	Standard Occupational Classification

| VA | Department of Veterans Affairs |
| WIA | The Workforce Investment Act of 1998 |

February, 28, 2014

Congressional Requesters

The aviation industry is vital to the U.S. economy, generating billions of dollars in revenue each year, providing employment, bolstering economic growth, and improving the quality of people's lives. In 2011, air transportation contributed almost $70 billion to the U.S. economy and accounted for over 450,000 jobs, according to the Bureau of Economic Analysis. Maintaining a safe and robust aviation system requires a sufficient number of qualified aviation professionals to design, manufacture, repair, and ensure the airworthiness of more than 225,000 civilian aircraft. While unforeseen events—including the terrorist attacks of September 2001 and the 2008 economic downturn—contributed to a downsizing of more than 100,000 jobs in the industry throughout the past decade, employment has increased in more recent years, and the industry is projecting a growth in demand for air travel and the number of aircraft manufactured.

Aviation stakeholders have expressed concern that an insufficient supply of certain types of aviation professionals–aerospace engineers, aircraft mechanics, and avionics technicians–could develop because of imminent retirements and a perception that fewer people are choosing to enter certain aviation professions. You asked that we review the current and projected future status of the professional aviation workforce. This report examines (1) what available data and forecasts reveal about the need for and potential availability of aerospace engineers, aircraft mechanics, and avionics technicians and (2) what actions industry and the federal government are taking, if any, to help attract and retain these professionals.[1]

This report looks specifically at three professions in the aviation industry—aerospace engineers, aircraft mechanics, and avionics technicians—which are involved in the design, manufacture, and repair of aircraft and have been the subject of concerns voiced by industry stakeholders. To examine current labor market conditions for these aviation professions, we analyzed data from the Bureau of Labor Statistics' (BLS) Current Population Survey (CPS) for years 2000 through 2012 on unemployment rates, employment numbers, and median weekly earnings (earnings)–referred to as "labor market indicators." We reviewed economic literature that describes how to evaluate labor market conditions that might indicate a labor shortage.[2] To understand the available workforce, we reviewed and analyzed data from the Department of Education (Education) on completion rates for degree or certificate programs that might prepare individuals to work in these professions from academic years 2000-2001 through 2011-2012; from the Department of Defense (DOD) on service members working in aviation maintenance separating from the military from fiscal year 2000 through 2012; and from the Federal Aviation Administration (FAA) on mechanic certificates issued from 2000 through 2012.[3] To assess the reliability of Education, DOD, and FAA data we reviewed documentation related to these data sources from our prior reports, agencies' websites, and interviewed knowledgeable government officials about the quality of the data. We determined the data to be sufficiently reliable for our purposes. We interviewed officials from seven select engineering, aviation maintenance technician (AMT), and avionics schools to understand training requirements and changes in demand for graduates. We selected training programs that varied based on location, size, and program specialty; our findings from these interviews should not be used to make generalizations about all training programs, but provide us with insights. We also reviewed studies that projected future demand for these professions and interviewed representatives of labor unions and industry associations. We did not verify the underlying data that these organizations collected and used in developing their projections of future demand. To understand the extent to which select employers have had difficulty attracting or retaining workers and any steps they have taken often to mitigate perceived shortages, we interviewed representatives and reviewed data from selected private companies that employ these professionals–including original equipment manufacturers (manufacturers); air carriers; and maintenance, repair, and overhaul facilities (repair stations). We selected 23 employers that ranged in size, geographic location, and type of work performed. Our findings from these interviews should not be used to make generalizations about all employers of these professionals, but provided us with insights. We also met with and reviewed documents from government officials, various industry groups that represent these professionals, and experts in labor economics to identify any actions taken or analyses that have been performed concerning these issues. See appendix I for more information about our scope and methodology and a listing of the employers we interviewed.

We conducted this performance audit from February 2013 through February 2014 in accordance with generally accepted government auditing standards. Those standards require that we plan and perform the audit to obtain sufficient, appropriate evidence to provide a reasonable basis for our findings and conclusions based on our audit objectives. We believe that the evidence obtained provides a reasonable basis for our findings and conclusions based on our audit objectives.

BACKGROUND

As noted, various aviation professionals are involved in the design, maintenance, and repair of aircraft and aircraft components (see fig. 1).

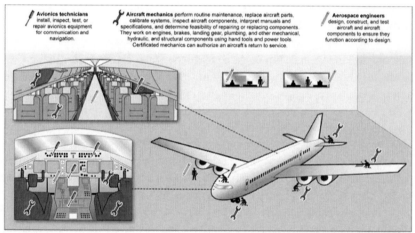

Source: GAO.

Figure 1. Examples of Tasks Performed by Selected Aviation Professionals.

These professionals are commonly employed by commercial air carriers, corporate flight departments, repair stations, or manufacturers of aircraft or aircraft components.

- Aerospace engineers working in aviation design aircraft and components, and test prototypes to make sure that they function according to design.[4] The vast majority of aerospace engineers have at least a bachelor's degree, according to BLS's Occupational Outlook Handbook.

- Aircraft mechanics inspect, service, and repair aircraft bodies (airframe) and engines (power plant). Aircraft mechanics can earn a mechanic certificate from FAA with either an airframe (A) rating, power plant (P) rating, or combined airframe and power plant (A&P) ratings, and are referred to as certificated mechanics. According to FAA data, almost all certificated mechanics (92 percent) hold A&P ratings. Applicants for a mechanic certificate must pass written and oral exams and demonstrate competence through a practical test. Certification is not necessary to work as an aircraft mechanic; however, without it, a mechanic cannot approve an aircraft for return to service and must be supervised by a certificated mechanic. Certificated mechanics that hold A&P ratings generally earn a higher wage and are more desirable to employers than mechanics who are not certificated, according to BLS.

  For an applicant to be authorized to take the mechanics examination for the combined A&P ratings, the applicant must either (1) complete an FAA-certificated AMT school; demonstrate and document relevant A&P work experience gained through on-the-job training, or (2) demonstrate and document work experience or some combination of work experience and education gained through the military working with airframes and engines.[5] Mechanics trained at an FAA-approved AMT school complete, at a minimum, 1900 curriculum hours of training: 750 curriculum hours in airframe subjects, 750 curriculum hours in power plant subjects, and 400 curriculum hours in general education subjects. Applicants seeking to take the mechanics examination for A&P ratings based on qualifying on-the-job training must provide documentary evidence of 30 months of practical experience concurrently performing the duties appropriate to the A&P ratings.[6]

- Avionics technicians test and troubleshoot aircraft instruments and components, install electronic components, and assemble switches or electrical controls. Avionics technicians receive training either through schooling, on the job, or in the military. Though some avionics technicians may hold a mechanics certificate, there is no FAA exam or certification specific to avionics technicians. However, some technicians seek certification from the Federal Communications Commission in the form of, for example, a General Radiotelephone Operator License.

Some avionics technicians may hold an A&P certificate or an FAA-issued repair-person certificate.[7] A repair-person certificate allows individuals to perform specific tasks at an FAA-certificated repair station, commercial operator, or air carrier that is authorized to perform those tasks.[8] Eligibility for a repair-person certificate requires employment by and recommendation from the FAA-approved employer. If an individual who holds a repair-person certificate leaves employment at that entity, he or she does not retain that certification.

Table 1 shows the employment levels, wages, and the largest type of employer for the aviation professions discussed in this report, as reported by BLS.

Table 1. Employment Levels and Salary Information for Selected Aviation Professions (2012)

Occupation	Total employment	Average hourly wage rate	Largest employertype
Aerospace engineer	80,420	$50.39	Manufacturing
Aircraft mechanic	119,160	$26.78	Air transportation support services[a]
Avionics technician	16,810	$26.65	Manufacturing

Source: BLS's Occupational Employment Statistics

[a]Air transportation support services include airport operation, servicing, repairing (except factory conversion and overhaul of aircraft), maintaining, and storing aircraft.

No single federal agency is tasked with developing the aviation workforce, but FAA is responsible for a variety of tasks related to developing and maintaining a qualified workforce. For example, FAA sets the minimum requirements for the academic curriculum and certifies and oversees AMT schools across the country.[9] With regard to certification of individual mechanics, FAA developed and administers the written A&P mechanic examination; certifies instructors (known as designated mechanic examiners) to administer the oral and practical tests to candidates; oversees the examiners; and issues A&P certificates to mechanics who successfully pass the examination. FAA also certifies and oversees repair stations within and outside of the United States and oversees maintenance performed by air carriers.[10] Several other federal agencies, including DOD, the Department of Veterans Affairs (VA), Education, and the Department of Labor (DOL), play a role in developing and maintaining a qualified aviation professional workforce, as shown in table 2.

Table 2. Examples of Agencies' Roles and Responsibilities Regarding Various Aviation Professionals

Agency	Role
FAA	FAA sets requirements and oversees the AMT schools and testing; issues certificates to mechanics and repair stations; and performs outreach on behalf of the profession.
DOD	DOD administers a training program meant to supplement work experience, which upon completion makes servicemembers eligible to take the mechanic certification exam.
VA	VA administers several programs to provide financial assistance for higher education.
DOL	DOL-supported workforce-training programs can fund engineering, mechanic, or avionics training programs.
BLS	BLS collects employment and wage data and makes long-term employment projections.
Education	Education provides financial assistance to support training in aviation-related fields.

Source: GAO analysis of government information.

The demand for air travel is highly sensitive to the state of the economy and to political, international, and even health-related events. As a result, despite periods of strong growth and earnings over the past decade, the industry has at times suffered substantial financial distress resulting in the industry contracting. For example, in response to the 2008 economic downturn and resulting decrease in demand for commercial air travel, airlines cut capacity and reduced their workforce. However, as demand for air travel has rebounded, the number of aircraft in operation and the size of the workforce are expected to grow. Representatives of the aviation industry are concerned there will not be a sufficient number of certain aviation professionals to support this growth—that is, the industry is concerned that the demand will exceed the available supply and that a labor shortage will result. While no agreed-upon definition for a labor shortage exists, it is commonly described as a sustained period during which the demand for workers in a geographic area exceeds the supply of workers available, qualified, and willing to work at a particular wage and under particular working conditions.

DATA AND FORECASTS PROVIDE MIXED EVIDENCE FOR A CURRENT OR FUTURE WORKFORCE SHORTAGE

Our analyses of labor market data indicate that a shortage of aerospace engineers may exist, but our analysis found less support for a shortage of aircraft mechanics.[11] For example, while both have low unemployment rates, neither employment nor earnings have increased for aircraft mechanics suggesting that employers' demand for this occupation has not outstripped supply. Stakeholders representing these groups also varied in their overall assessment of the labor market. Further, while some of these individuals will pursue other careers, the number of people completing degrees in these or related fields has increased in recent years, and BLS employment projections indicate slower than average or no growth through 2022.

Evidence Is Mixed for a Current Shortage of Selected Aviation Professionals

While no single metric can be used to identify whether a labor shortage exists, labor market data can be used as "indicators" —in conjunction with observations from stakeholders.[12] According to economic literature, one can look at historical unemployment rates, as well as trends in employment and earnings.[13] If a labor shortage were to exist, one would expect a low unemployment rate signaling limited availability of workers in a profession; increases in employment due to demand for that occupation increasing; and increases in wages offered to draw more people into the industry.[14] Of these three indicators, the unemployment rate provides the most direct measure of a labor shortage because it estimates the number of people who are unemployed and actively looking for work in a specific occupation.[15] The other indicators can be affected by factors unrelated to a labor shortage; for example, wages may be determined by union contracts rather than market demand. Results of these indicators can be analyzed in relation to other occupations and by using absolute scales defined by benchmarks that we identified in the economic literature.[16]

Table 3. Unemployment, Employment, and Earnings for Selected Aviation Professions, 2000–2012

Occupation	Unemployment		Change in full-time employment (as a percentage per year)		Change in median weekly earnings (as a percentage per year)	
	Rate (average)	Rank (total 295)	Rate (yearly)	Rank (total 490)	Rate (yearly)	Rank (total 250)
Aerospace engineers	2.3[a]	38	4.6[a]	45	0.3	60
Aircraft mechanics and service technicians	3.0[a]	70	-0.25	265	-0.07	127
All occupations	6.3	N/A	0.1	N/A	0.06	N/A

Source: GAO analysis of BLS's CPS data.

Notes: Data are from unpublished CPS tables.

Average annual unemployment rates were ranked from lowest to highest. Yearly rates of change in full-time employment were ranked from highest to lowest. Yearly changes in earnings were ranked from highest to lowest.

BLS adopted the Standard Occupational Classification (SOC) titles in 2010. As a result, some occupations were combined and others were phased out. While this did not affect the occupations relevant to our analysis, it affected the total number of occupations. We excluded any occupation for which the name changed. We also excluded occupations for an indicator if BLS did not report unemployment, or median weekly earnings, or employment for any year. We excluded avionics technicians since the workforce included fewer than 50,000 people and BLS did not report unemployment in many years.

In the table, growth rates for the change in employment and earnings were calculated by fitting a time trend using a log linear regression, for which we computed statistical significance. As such, our calculations yield different larger annual changes compared to calculating the percent change over the same time period and annualizing the percent change, because our method does not include the effect of compounding. For example, the 51 percent change over the 12 year period for aerospace engineers would result in a 3.6 annual rate of change, as opposed to the 4.6 reported in the table. This would be the largest difference of any numbers reported in the table.

[a]Denotes that the indicator would be suggestive of a labor shortage, although not at the highest level.

Two of the three labor market indicators we examined for aerospace engineers suggest that the profession may be experiencing a labor shortage (see table 3). From 2000 through 2012, the unemployment rate for aerospace engineers has averaged 2.3 percent—much lower than the economy as a whole—and employment has increased by about 50 percent.[17] Both the unemployment rate and employment could be suggestive of a labor shortage relative to other occupations and based on the scale we identified in the economic literature. For example, over this period, aerospace engineers had the 38th (out of 295) lowest unemployment rate and 45th (out of 490) largest growth in employment.[18] Similarly, according to the 7-point scale we identified in economic literature, the unemployment rate and employment growth would receive a 5, which is not the highest rating, but still provides some support for a labor shortage.[19] Median earnings for aerospace engineers, however, have stayed about the same over that time period, a statistic that does not appear consistent with a labor shortage.[20] Specifically, if employers were experiencing difficulty hiring aerospace engineers, one would expect earnings to rise to attract new workers to the industry. However, other factors can also account for a lack of growth in earnings even during a labor shortage. For example, earnings may be slow to adjust to other labor market trends, or certain aspects of an industry may prevent wages from increasing (e.g., a highly competitive industry with slim profit margins). Furthermore, over our analytical time period, wages were stagnant through much of the economy as a result of two economic downturns.

Data for aircraft mechanics provide less evidence of a labor shortage. From 2000 through 2012, the average unemployment rate for aircraft mechanics has been 3 percent—about half the rate for the entire workforce—which could be suggestive of a labor shortage.[21] However, earnings for aircraft mechanics remained static and employment decreased.[22] Industry stakeholders varied in their assessment of the labor market. Some industry officials we spoke with, representing companies that employ aircraft mechanics across the United States, told us that the industry was currently experiencing a labor shortage; however, others believed that there were enough people to perform the work, but companies were competing to hire the most experienced personnel. According to one industry stakeholder we spoke, the major airlines are not having difficulty attracting workers. As another stakeholder explained, if difficulty existed attracting workers, smaller businesses, and general aviation—particularly in rural areas—would most likely be affected first. The low unemployment rate suggests that with few available people to hire, employers may have difficulty finding people with specific skill sets, certifications, or work experiences.

Our analysis of labor market data has a number of limitations given the nature of the CPS data from BLS and the scope of our analysis. SOC titles are broad, and may not take into account specific requirements an employer seeks. For example, many employers may require employees to hold an A&P certificate. However, BLS's occupational classification for aircraft mechanics includes both certificated and non-certificated mechanics. As a result, labor market data may overestimate the number of available mechanics for certain employers. Moreover, BLS only publicly reports annual employment data for occupations that have at least 50,000 people; as a result, we were unable to analyze data for avionics technicians. We identified the following other limitations of the labor market indicators:

- Data are collected through a household survey and are subject to sampling and response errors. Often, one individual will identify occupation, employment, and wage data for all household members; individuals may report incorrect or inconsistent information.
- Survey results of unemployment rates are based on the person's last job, rather than the longest job held or occupation in which a person is trained or looking for work: the data, therefore, can miss individuals who are seeking work in a particular occupation. For example, an A&P mechanic who lost a job, worked temporarily in the automotive industry, and was then seeking employment as an A&P mechanic, would be classified as an automotive mechanic not as an A&P mechanic, when surveyed by BLS.
- BLS reports data on median earnings for aviation professionals in all stages of their careers, so we could not examine whether starting earnings have increased, an examination that would be more likely to indicate if wages were rising to attract entry-level workers.
- The data were collected at a national level; while not all indicators were consistent with a labor shortage, our analysis would not identify any regional shortages.
- Research by BLS and others suggests job vacancy data as another potential indicator for identifying labor shortages. However, BLS does not collect information on job vacancies at the occupational level. Job vacancy data are collected by some states and private companies, but the data are limited. We could not obtain complete and

sufficiently reliable occupational-level job-vacancy data from these sources.[23]

Finally, as mentioned above, no single measure can provide definitive evidence as to whether a labor shortage exists. Rather, these data can indicate the extent to which employers may have difficulty attracting people at the current wage rate. Moreover, even if perfect data existed, the term labor shortage is sometimes used to describe a variety of situations, some of which are generally not considered to be shortages.[24] For example, during periods of economic recession, employers may become accustomed to hiring a high caliber of candidate with specific training or levels of experience at a prescribed wage rate. In these cases, employers can be more selective when hiring candidates and could, for example, look for individuals with niche skills or more experience. However, during an economic expansion, where companies may be increasing the size of their workforce, it is likely that the number of job applicants will shrink and employers may have difficulty finding the same caliber of candidate. Under these circumstances, the employer's challenge may become one of quality of available people, not necessarily quantity of people willing and able to do the job.

Data Suggest That the Number of Individuals in the Selected Professions Is Increasing, but Several Industries Compete for These Workers

From 2000 through 2012, the number of people identifying as aerospace engineers and aircraft mechanics and service technicians–both certificated and non-certificated–has increased, according to BLS data (see fig. 2).[25] For example, the size of the aircraft-mechanic and service- technician workforce in 2012 had increased 5 percent since 2000. Moving forward, a couple stakeholders that represent training programs and members of the armed services noted that they expect an increase in the number of available mechanics due to an increase in the number of completions in aircraft maintenance related degrees and people separating from the armed services, respectively.

The number of completions in aerospace-engineering-related fields has generally increased, according to data from Education.[26] For example, from academic years 2000–2001 through 2011–2012, there has been a 39 percent increase in the number of completions (see fig. 3).

Representatives from engineering programs we spoke with generally suggested that the number of completions from engineering programs will be sufficient to meet demand given future BLS employment projections. Therefore, they suggested that it is unlikely that a labor shortage will develop in the near future. For example, one representative told us he would expect demand to be met given the increase in the number of completions combined with the projected slow growth in government projections for selected employment in the aviation field. The same stakeholder noted that the vast majority of engineers are getting employment offers, but are receiving, on average, fewer offers than in past years. A union representative we spoke with echoed a similar sentiment, saying that aerospace engineering needs will be met given the number of engineers entering the workforce.

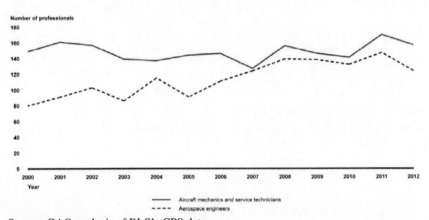

Source: GAO analysis of BLS's CPS data.
Note: Data are not available for avionics technicians because the survey sample size is too small for data to meet the reporting threshold.

Figure 2. Number of Aerospace Engineers and Aircraft Mechanics, 2000–2012 (in thousands).

Numbers of aerospace engineering completions, however, are not a direct reflection of the number of individuals entering the aviation workforce. According to FAA, the industry also uses civil, software, and chemical engineers, among others. For example, the aviation industry requires electrical and software engineers to design airplane motors or electrical circuits and design programs to make air travel faster, respectively. Further, other industries, such as financial services and information technology, compete for aerospace and other types of engineers and often offer less career uncertainty and more exciting job prospects, according to one industry stakeholder representing aerospace companies. Officials we spoke with both at engineering training programs and within industry attributed this to the fact that the aviation industry is highly cyclical, offering less job security than other industries.

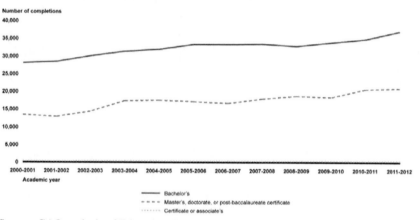

Source: GAO analysis of Education data.

Note: Analysis includes degree programs that train individuals for work as aerospace engineers.

Figure 3. Completions in Aerospace-Engineering-Related Fields by Level of Degree, 2001–2012.

In terms of the other aviation occupations, the number of completions of AMT-related programs has also increased; however, the number of completions in avionics related programs has not.[27] Over the past decade, the number of students receiving degrees in aircraft maintenance has increased by 48 percent (see fig. 4), while the number of students receiving degrees in avionics has decreased by 53 percent. However, data on degrees granted in avionics may not be a good indicator for the number of people gaining training to be an avionics technician. For example, according to officials from one school, a sizeable portion of avionics technicians received training in other fields, including electronics technology or electrical engineering, which is not captured in these data. Similarly, some AMT schools offer avionics specialties; though students may go on to be avionics technicians, according to this data source, they are classified as aircraft mechanics. According to officials from a couple selected AMT schools, based on the number of students enrolled in avionics specialties in their schools, interest in avionics has increased in recent years.

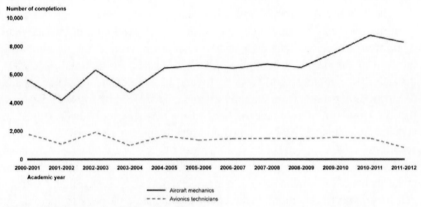

Source: GAO analysis of Education data.
Note: Analysis includes degree programs that train individuals for work as aircraft
    mechanics or avionics technicians.

Figure 4. Aircraft-Mechanic and Avionics-Maintenance-Related Completions, 2001–2012.

Nevertheless, we heard from education officials at selected AMT and avionics schools and others that not all graduating students received job offers or go to work in the aviation industry upon completion. For example, officials at the majority of AMT schools we visited told us that graduates on occasion pursue other fields of work. According to these officials, some graduates from AMT schools pursue other occupations that offer higher wages or better working conditions—such as the industrial heating industry—or occupations that are likely considered more exciting such as working for amusement parks and NASCAR (National Association for Stock Car Auto Racing, Inc.). Some officials suggested this could be a result of students not yet earning an A&P certificate. However, this also could suggest there are more students entering the field than jobs available in a particular location or that employers are hesitant to hire A&P mechanics directly out of school.

Enrollments at AMT schools have generally been increasing and, if demand existed, AMT schools could train more people to become aircraft mechanics and avionics technicians. According to the Aviation Technician Education Council, an organization that represents more than 100 AMT schools, 10 of those reported that they were, on average, utilizing about half of their training capacity.[28] This is similar to what we were told by 3 of the 5 schools we interviewed, which reported that they could or planned to increase capacity.

The number of aircraft mechanics and avionics technicians separating from the military—another main source of supply—and entering the civilian workforce has stayed relatively constant since fiscal year 2001, but will likely increase in the future, according to DOD officials.[29] From fiscal year 2001 through 2012, about 16,000 workers trained in aviation maintenance related occupations separated from the military annually, according to DOD data (see fig. 5). However, it is unknown how many of these individuals stayed in aviation maintenance upon completion of their military service. Further, according to DOD officials, the vast majority of these individuals will not hold an A&P certificate when entering the civilian workforce, a factor that can make them less desirable to employers. Nevertheless, DOD officials told us that they expect separations for aviation maintenance workers to increase in the future given planned workforce reductions.

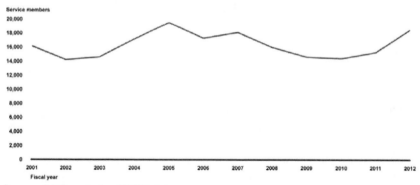

Source: GAO analysis of DOD data.

Figure 5. Aviation Maintenance Personnel Annually Separating from the Military, Fiscal Years 2001–2012.

The annual number of newly issued A&P certificates, while declining in the early 2000's and staying relatively constant at about 6,000 new certificates annually from 2003 to 2010, has increased in recent years (see fig. 6). About 7,000 individuals were issued their certificates in 2012. These individuals met the requirements either through attending AMT schools (4,072) or through on-the-job training or military service training (2,824). Over this same period, the pool of certificated A&P mechanics has stayed roughly the same, according to

FAA—ranging from roughly 313,000 to 338,000 individuals. In 2013, there were over 335,000 certificated A&P mechanics age 70 or younger.

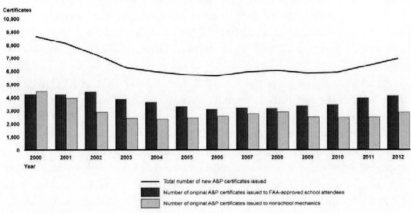

Source: GAO analysis of FAA data.

Figure 6. The Number of New A&P Certificates Issued by Training Type, 2000–2012.

Projections Suggest Slower Than Average or No Growth for the Selected Aviation Professions

BLS's employment projections suggest slower than average or no growth for our selected professions over the next 10 years.[30] From 2012 to 2022, according to BLS, the U.S. economy is projected to add more than 15.6 million new jobs as total employment grows from nearly 145.4 million to more than 161 million (an overall 10.8 percent growth rate or an annualized growth rate of 1.0 percent per year). According to BLS, the number of aerospace engineers employed in the United States is projected to increase to 89,100 by 2022, an overall 7.3 percent increase over the 83,000 employed in 2012.[31] Alternatively, employment for aircraft mechanics and service technicians and for avionics technicians employed in the United States is projected to show little or no change through 2022. Employment for aircraft mechanics and services technicians and avionics technicians is expected to increase by about 2.5 percent (or 3,000 jobs) and 2.9 percent (or 500 jobs) over the same 10-year period, respectively.[32] While air traffic is expected to increase over the coming decade, according to BLS, it is likely that airlines' continued outsourcing of maintenance overseas and the introduction of newer aircraft that require less maintenance will affect demand for these occupations. While projections show slower than average or no growth for these occupations, BLS also provides forecasts of the number of job openings to accommodate both industry growth and the replacement of workers leaving these jobs.[33] According to BLS data, most of the demand for new workers in these three occupations will be to replace those retiring or leaving the profession.

BLS's future employment demand for an industry or occupation is influenced by the projected demand for goods and services produced by an industry. For example, the projected employment of aircraft mechanics and service technicians is influenced by the projected demand for air travel and various manufacturing industries. To estimate future employment in the various occupations, BLS uses historical economic and employment data and forecasts of key economic factors, such as economic growth by sector of the economy, to estimate the number of jobs that will result in those industries.

While BLS's projections are helpful in gaining a sense of the expected growth in aviation employment, developing long-term occupational employment projections is inherently uncertain for a variety of reasons. Specifically, these projections rely on a set of assumptions about the future, some of which may not come to fruition. For example, BLS's projection assumes a full-employment economy in the target year, but if a recession occurred, for example, projections for employment are likely to be overstated. That said, projecting occupational employment is reasonably feasible because there are often historical data showing employment trends that can be compared to, for example, economic growth and factors affecting the airline industry—including trends in passenger travel and the cost of key inputs, such as fuel. On the other hand, analyzing whether a shortage might arise in an occupation would require an understanding of both the supply and demand characteristics of the market and an ability to project each of these relationships independently. The factors underlying those relationships require information that is more detailed and likely difficult to develop based on past data, a challenge exacerbated when projecting into the future. For example, forecasting the labor supply requires understanding how the number of people who might choose to work in an occupation varies at different wage rates or working conditions. In the case of the three selected professions, we have past data on the trends in the number of degrees or certifications awarded—which tend to show a growing number of people entering the professions—but these data do not provide a forecast of future supply. Nonetheless, with employment growth projected to be slower than average or not to grow and recent trends indicating a stable or growing supply of personnel, there is little reason to believe that a significant shortage is likely to arise in the United States over the next several years.

INDUSTRY AND GOVERNMENT ARE TAKING SOME ACTIONS TO FACILITATE ENTRY INTO THE AVIATION WORKFORCE, BUT EMPLOYERS REMAIN CONCERNED ABOUT FUTURE NEEDS

Most of the employers we interviewed reported some challenges hiring individuals in the selected professions; often this was not an issue of an insufficient number of candidates seeking employment, but rather an insufficient number of candidates with the experience and skills employers sought available to work at the wage being offered. Certain employers, for example those seeking niche or craft skills or those located far from metropolitan areas, cited particular difficulty attracting workers. Almost all employers we spoke with reported taking some actions that economists associate with responding to a labor shortage, but few were raising wages to attract workers. Federal agencies have programs in place that support training for the selected aviation professions, but employers of all sizes, including those that are not currently experiencing hiring challenges, were concerned that young people are losing interest in aviation careers and that future employment needs may go unmet.

Employers Reported Varying Levels of Difficulty Filling Vacancies and Attracting Individuals in the Selected Aviation Professions

Most of the employers we interviewed—particularly the small and medium-sized firms—cited some challenges hiring individuals in the selected aviation professions with the skills they were seeking at the wage they offered. Of the 23 employers we interviewed, 16 expressed some degree of difficulty hiring, though often the issue was not due to an insufficient number of workers, but rather an insufficient number of workers with the experience levels employers desired. Employers also reported challenges hiring mechanics with certain niche or craft skills, such as upholstery, welding, and cabinetry—skills that are not unique to aviation. Similarly, employers seeking aerospace engineers, as well as mechanical and electrical engineers, reported difficulty filling vacancies. According to some employers and stakeholders we interviewed, attracting engineers is made difficult by the lack of job security that results from the cyclical nature of the aerospace industry and the volatility of demand for aircraft and air travel related to the economy.

Certain employers also cited location as a challenge to attracting individuals in our selected professions. For example, employers located farther from metropolitan areas or those considered to be "aviation hubs" explained that they had difficulty attracting people for engineering and mechanic positions. Employers seeking to hire mechanics added that in more rural areas, they would have the most success hiring and retaining employees from the surrounding areas, but have found it difficult to do so if there is not a local AMT school to support training needs.

Smaller employers—those with less than 100 employees—often considered themselves to be at a disadvantage in attracting workers relative to larger companies. According to 5 of these 13 employers, large air carriers and major manufacturers are considered more desirable, offering employees a sense of stability and an air of prestige, often at higher wages. Employment with an air carrier also offers attractive fringe benefits, such as the ability to fly on standby or for a discounted fare. One employer we interviewed, which is collocated at an airport with a repair station for a large manufacturer, said that despite its offer of comparable wages, it has a hard time competing with the brand-name recognition of larger employers. Consistent with this assessment, more than half of the large employers we interviewed said that they were not currently experiencing difficulties attracting and retaining workers.

Employers who reported challenges hiring A&P mechanics often expressed a reluctance to hire recent graduates or recently certificated A&P mechanics. While the A&P certificate may signal an aptitude and a level of general knowledge, many employers felt that recent graduates lack on-the-job experiences to supplement their education. According to employers, it generally takes between 1 and 3 years to become fully proficient as a mechanic. As a result, according to 5 of the 23 employers who provided their opinions, preferred employment candidates were generally certificated A&P mechanics with at least 2 to 5 years of experience working with the specific aircraft types that the employer maintained and repaired because these individuals could make an immediate contribution with limited supervision.

While employers found the A&P curriculum to generally be well-aligned, overall, with their needs, some employers we interviewed said that the curriculum's focus is on out-dated technologies—such as aircraft built with dope and fabric—at the expense of more relevant topics, such as composite materials. We previously reported similar concerns from industry stakeholders in 2003.[34] Specifically, at that time stakeholders indicated that the core curriculum at AMT schools provided mechanics with a solid understanding of basic repair principles, but that some parts of the curriculum were obsolete and covered aspects of aviation repair that are rarely needed or used by A&P mechanics.[35] At least two of those areas—soldering and welding—have been identified by researchers as subjects that could be deleted or condensed because of infrequency of use. However, employers we interviewed indicated skills in these areas were lacking among the current workforce, especially recently certificated A&P mechanics. Given the diversity in the type and age of aircraft in the civilian fleet, satisfying the needs of all employers would be difficult. For example, while dope and fabric aircraft are less common, some certificated aircraft are still produced with those materials; and while composite materials are being used in new airframe construction, aluminum airframes are still the most common.

In addition to challenges hiring workers, 7 of the 23 companies we interviewed reported that while they had some difficulties retaining employees, overall retention was not a major issue. That said, according to representatives of these companies, most of the employees who resign leave for similar positions at companies that offer higher wages, that are located in places with a lower cost of living, or that are considered to be employers that are more attractive. Nevertheless, some leave for other industries. According to some employers and stakeholders we spoke to, mechanics have relevant skills for working at a variety of occupations, including at amusement parks or on oil rigs, which were stated to be either higher paying or have characteristics employees found more favorable.

Employers Are Taking a Variety of Actions to Attract and Retain Individuals in the Selected Aviation Professions

According to economic literature we reviewed, employers—who first identify a shortage when they encounter difficulty filling vacancies at the current wage rate—may take a variety of actions in response to a perceived labor shortage.[36] Their actions vary in desirability for the employer based on resources required and their permanency. For example, increasing recruiting requires fewer resources than investing in technologies that could replace labor; further, recruitment efforts could be halted if labor market conditions changed, whereas investing in new technologies cannot be easily undone. Employers may also choose to take some of these actions for reasons other than filling vacancies—for example, to improve morale among current employees or to increase profitability.

In response to difficulties filling employment vacancies, employers may:

- *Increase recruiting efforts.* Increasing recruiting efforts includes such activities as increasing advertising, using public or private employment agencies, and paying recruiting bonuses to employees who refer new hires.
- *Increase the use of overtime.* Employers may choose to have current employees work additional hours in place of hiring additional workers, especially if they do not expect hiring difficulties to last for a substantial period of time.
- *Reduce the minimum qualifications for the job.* Employers may have set minimum qualifications higher than necessary and may choose to reduce those qualifications when hiring becomes difficult. Though employers cannot reduce the requirements for earning A&P certification, they may choose to hire non-certificated mechanics or lower required years of experience necessary for consideration for employment.
- *Restructure the work to use current or new employees in other occupations.* In some cases, complex jobs can be decomposed into simpler tasks, allowing less-skilled and perhaps cheaper labor to be used in place of other occupations. For example, employers may choose to use less-skilled workers to begin the repair process by pulling panels from aircraft, freeing A&P mechanics for other tasks.
- *Substitute machinery and equipment for labor.* Employers may sometimes be able to use machinery or equipment in place of labor. For example, a die-cut machine can precisely cut sheet metal, a task that was previously done by hand.
- *Train workers for the job.* In a difficult labor market, an employer that traditionally relied upon colleges or vocational or trade schools to train its workforce may choose to offer or sponsor training.
- *Improve working conditions.* Improving working conditions—such as changes in hours worked, equipment or facility upgrades, training,

and job recognition efforts—may be a means to attract and retain workers.

- *Offer bonuses to new employees.* Employers may offer new employees a "signing" bonus, such as, covering moving expenses for agreeing to join a company.
- *Improve wages and fringe benefits.* Increasing wages will help increase the number of workers willing to work in a particular position or occupation. However, employers are reluctant to do this because they may be forced to raise the wages of current employees as well. Further, unlike some other actions, once wages are raised, it is unlikely that they will be reduced later if hiring becomes less difficult.
- *Contract out the work.* If employers cannot fill vacancies for employees in certain occupations, it may contract out those tasks to another firm.
- *Turn down work.* If a firm has exhausted other means to mitigate its hiring challenges and vacancies persist, it may choose to turn down work.

Companies we interviewed took some of the above actions in direct response to a perceived labor shortage. For example, 10 of the 16 companies that reported hiring difficulties increased recruiting efforts— including using social media and attending career fairs. Many companies also made use of specialty websites that advertise aviation jobs as well as staffing and recruiting agencies that offer short-term contract workers and contract-to-hire options. Almost half of the companies we interviewed—including those that did not cite challenges hiring—also developed and leveraged relationships with local schools as a means to recruit workers. According to one company, its location made attracting employees difficult and there were no local schools from which to recruit. In response, it built a relationship with a local technical college with an automotive-maintenance-training program and hired and trained its students—with aptitude in painting and certain machinery—for related aviation tasks.

Almost all companies we interviewed reported training workers for the job, though few reported providing the initial training to become a mechanic, instead many offered A&P mechanics they employed the opportunity for training in areas specific to the work they were doing for the company. For example, 18 of the 22 companies that reported providing training to its employees sent employees to training courses specific to the make or model of aircraft that the company repaired, or to courses that would build company capabilities on topics such as composites or non-destructive testing. Only one company we interviewed reported hiring individuals without formal training, training them on-the-job, and paying for their A&P testing. Another company reported hiring former military members and sending them for refresher courses to prepare them for the A&P certification exam.

Approximately one-third of companies reported reducing their minimum standards for employment. For example, three companies lowered the number of years of experience it required of applicants and another said that it would like to do so in the future to expand its hiring pool. However, 10 of the companies we interviewed said they would not lower standards; they reasoned that doing so might reduce the quality of their work and they were not willing to expose themselves or their clients to those risks, or that doing so would, in the end, be more expensive for them because non-certificated mechanics need to be under the supervision of a certificated mechanic. Nine of the companies we interviewed that had challenges attracting workers also reported having to turn down work because of staffing constraints, though the frequency varied. According to some of these companies, turning down work was a last resort. In addition, in some instances, companies described receiving requests for services that they could not accommodate in the customer's desired time frames, and as a result, the customer went elsewhere.

Few companies we interviewed reported raising wages, improving benefits, or offering bonuses to attract employees. Five of the 16 companies that reported difficulties filling vacancies also raised wages. However, only one did so explicitly to attract additional mechanics; two did so to remain competitive with other employers, one did so following a multi-year pay freeze, and the last raised wages after it was acquired by a larger entity. Four companies that reported difficulties filling vacancies offered bonuses to new employees. Though raising wages and offering bonuses would be obvious ways to increase the number of workers willing to work in a particular occupation, doing so could have implications in the market for air travel or aircraft repair if those costs are passed on to the customer. The inability to pass those costs on was the reason that officials from at least one company we interviewed provided for why the company could not afford to raise wages; according to that company, its clients—air carriers—paid a fixed amount, leaving no margin for increased labor costs. In other situations, companies facing competition from repair stations abroad where labor is cheaper may also find it difficult to increase wages.

Officials from many of the companies we interviewed were taking some of the actions we identified for reasons unrelated to difficulty filling vacancies.

For example, 17 of the companies we interviewed indicated that they used overtime but not necessarily in place of hiring additional workers. According to those employers, the nature of their business is such that there are peaks and valleys in workflow. At times, the amount of work that must be completed is in excess of what can be completed in a normal workweek; however, it is not a sustained level of work and hiring additional employees would mean layoffs or having to cut hours at other points in the year. Eighteen companies also indicated that they improved working conditions—such as by improving the tools available to employees, updating safety mechanisms, and installing fans or lighting to making working in hangars more comfortable—in efforts to improve morale and retention.

Some actions were taken largely in response to business needs. For example, almost all of the companies we interviewed reported contracting out some tasks that were more economical than building the capabilities to complete them internally. These tasks included non-destructive testing and parts plating. In addition, approximately half of companies we interviewed discussed restructuring their work as a means to maximize efficiency. According to those companies, they did not necessarily restructure their work in an effort reduce the number of mechanics or engineers required in response to or because of hiring challenges. Instead, they sought to maximize the efficiency of their current workforce by using more experienced mechanics to do work that is more complicated. Further, while approximately one-third of the companies we interviewed reported introducing technologies to improve efficiency in the workplace—for example, automating the troubleshooting part of repair work—only one company substituted the use of machinery (a die-cut machine) for positions previously held by people.

The Federal Government Maintains Several Programs and Initiatives That Can Help Attract People to Aviation-Related Fields

As mentioned previously, while no single agency is tasked with developing the aviation professional workforce, several maintain programs that help promote and train people for aviation-related careers. At the time of its creation in 1958, the FAA was tasked with regulating, promoting, encouraging, and developing civil aeronautics. In 1996, following criticism of its response to the ValuJet crash in the Florida Everglades and to address concerns about its dual role, FAA's mission was amended to make ensuring the safety of the national air-space system the agency's top priority.[37] According to FAA, it remained responsible for promotional tasks, but specific references were deleted from its mandate.

Currently, FAA's Office of Aviation and Space Education (AVSED) is tasked with increasing the public's knowledge of aviation and the key role air transportation plays in the U.S. economy, and serves to help recruit new workers into the field. AVSED collaborates with federal, state, and local agencies, as well as private sector entities, to promote aviation-related science, technology, engineering, and math (STEM) skills and grow the pipeline of students seeking to work in aerospace-related fields or aviation maintenance. To this end, AVSED produced a DVD and developed a brochure on aviation maintenance careers that it shares with college recruiters and high school guidance counselors and distributes at career fairs, and that has been shown on public television. AVSED also ran a national poster campaign called, "Yes I Can Do That." In partnership with other organizations, AVSED is involved in a variety of activities, including the *Real World Design Challenge*, a high school-level engineering competition; the *Build-a-Plane* program which provides schools with aircraft to be used as teaching tools; and the *Walk in my Boots Program*, which offers students the opportunity to observe aviation mechanics in the hangar for a day. In addition, AVSED works with the Centers of Excellence, which award aerospace research grants to colleges and the National Coalition of Certification Centers, a network of education providers and corporations that supports and advances technology skills in the aviation industry, among others, and promotes aviation-maintenance technical degrees and careers. Further, AVSED maintains national partnerships with various groups with shared interest in growing the aviation workforce, including the Organization of Black Aerospace Professionals, Women in Aviation International, Youth Aviation Adventure, and the Experimental Aircraft Association.

AVSED tries to track the number of events it organizes and individuals who participate; however, it does not have a mechanism to evaluate the effectiveness of those programs or if the participants pursue an aviation-related career. Without a measure of effectiveness or feedback mechanism to determine if the materials are reaching AVSED's target audience and if that audience is responsive to its efforts, FAA may be missing opportunities to improve performance.[38] However, according to AVSED officials, efforts to track program participation and outcomes would be difficult from a privacy perspective given the ages of its target audience and would be prohibitively costly to execute. AVSED's outreach efforts are done with limited funding as the office does not have a dedicated budget; instead, AVSED relies on transfers from other offices for its activities. For example, the DVD and brochures it produced were made with funds transferred from Flight Standards.

Other agencies also administer programs that could encourage entry into aviation careers.

- *DOD* trains and employs over 114,000 individuals working in occupations that are comparable to the aviation professional occupations discussed in this report. However, while in the military, mechanics are not mandated to hold A&P certificates. Further, their training may be for specific tasks or duties and, as a result, does not necessarily qualify them for eligibility to take the A&P exam. As previously mentioned, though certification is not required for civilian employment either, certificated A&P mechanics can command higher wages and have better promotion potential.

In an effort to help separating service members find civilian employment and to promote a more professional military workforce, DOD has undertaken several actions to facilitate A&P certification of its members. For example, since 2002 the Community College of the Air Force has run the FAA-approved JSAMTCC bridge program that, upon completion, confers a certificate of eligibility—equivalent to a training program diploma—to take the A&P exam. The JSAMTCC program is available to members of all services who have attained minimum requirements in aviation maintenance—typically after 3 years of experience in a related position—and includes three self-paced courses taken online in addition to on-the-job training. According to DOD officials, depending on individual circumstances, the time to complete the program varies. According to DOD, several thousand service members have enrolled in the program (see table 4). However, the numbers who have completed the program are much smaller, likely because deployments and other activities interrupt coursework. Once eligible for the exam, service members can complete the written portions of the A&P exam free at testing facilities located on base. In addition, the Navy, for example, subsidizes the cost of the practical and oral exams for its members and the Army awards promotion points for attainment of the certification. In coordination with the FAA, the services have also standardized their forms to facilitate proving eligibility to take the exam.

**Table 4. Aircraft-Maintenance-Technician Certification Program
Enrollments and Completions by Service, 2002–2013**

	Air Force	Army	Marine Corps	Navy	Coast Guard
Enrolled	5,911	1,916	145	1,274	16
Completions	193	39	7	39	14

Source: DOD.

In the last year, DOD also completed a pilot program aimed at streamlining credentialing and licensing for military members that included aircraft mechanics.[39] The Navy and Air Force, which employ the largest number of aircraft mechanics, participated by designing efforts to increase participation in the technician certification program. DOD found that though it would be ideal for service members to start the program early in their military careers, service members lacked an appreciation for the differences between the military and civilian requirements for aircraft mechanics, and for the value of FAA certification, resulting in many choosing not to participate.[40] The services also found that the cost of taking the A&P exam—on average $1,750—was prohibitively expensive for some who completed the JSAMTCC program. As part of the pilot program, the Air Force made arrangements to pay the fee. The Navy, which already had a program in place to meet the cost of certification exams, focused on better marketing for the program. Based on the outcomes of their efforts, the Navy plans to continue outreach and the Air Force plans to pay for all exam costs, funding permitting.

In coordination with DOL, VA, and other federal partners, DOD also administers the Transition Assistance Program (TAP) [41] for eligible separating service members. TAP consists of a 5-day core curriculum with segments on translating military skills to civilian job requirements, financial planning, and individual counseling and assessment with the goal of each service member's developing an individual transition plan. It also includes a process that "crosswalks" military jobs to civilian occupations by evaluating the transferability of skills from the individual's military occupational specialty to civilian occupations. In addition, participants may attend one or more 2-day tracks, including tracks focused on entering a technical skills training program. Moving forward, DOD has said that it plans to shift to a Military Life Cycle Transition Model by October 2014, a more proactive approach intended to integrate transition preparation—counseling, assessments, and access to resources to build skills or credentials— throughout the course of a service member's military career. Federal laws, as well as DOD policy, generally require that eligible transitioning service members participate in many components of TAP; DOD's annual goal is for 90 percent of eligible separating service members to attend the mandatory TAP components.[42]

- *The Post 9/11 GI Bill*, established in 2008 and available through VA, provides full tuition and fees for all public school in-state students and reimbursement for private institutions of higher learning for up to $19,198 per academic year.[43] It is currently VA's largest education program. Financial support provides up to 36 months of education benefits, which are generally payable for 15 years following release from active duty. Though the program distributed more than $8.5 billion in tuition, housing, and other payments in fiscal year 2012, we have previously found that problems with its administration and delays in payment create financial challenges for student veterans.[44] We made recommendations to VA to address these problems, and VA has taken steps to respond to those recommendations, including efforts related to educating student veterans about education benefits prior to enrollment and working with postsecondary schools to identify information to facilitate timely access to other sources of federal financial aid while VA benefits were processed. Additional benefits are also available to veterans with higher expenses through the "Yellow Ribbon Program."

- *Education* offers grants, work-study funds, and low interest loans to help cover expenses such as tuition and fees, books and supplies, and room and board, as well as other related expenses. Schools that offer training in aviation-related fields are eligible for this funding. (See table 5 for information on the number of students majoring in aviation-related fields receiving aid and the total amount of aid received.) We did not identify any funding sources that specifically targeted the selected aviation professions discussed in this report.

- *DOL:* Under the Workforce Investment Act of 1998 (WIA) administered by DOL[45] , training services are available to eligible individuals who meet requirements for services—including training to become an aerospace engineer, aircraft mechanic, or avionics technician. To be eligible for training support, individuals must first participate in what are considered core services—job search and placement assistance—and intensive services—individual employment and career plans. WIA does not specify an amount of time one must spend or the number of attempts one must make to gain employment before moving to the next level in the sequence of services, and the state-level administrators of the moneys have discretion on how much is spent on training relative to other services. Due to the limited sum of money available, WIA requires that individuals receiving training funds be unable to obtain grant funding from other sources to pay the cost of training.[46] According to DOL, workforce counselors encourage those interested to seek support from other sources (including VA and Education) prior to seeking WIA training funds. WIA funds were used in whole or in part to support training in aviation-related fields for more than 2,000 individuals from 2010 through 2012.[47]

Table 5. Number of and Amount of Aid Disbursed to Students Majoring in Aviation-Related Fields Receiving Federal Aid, 2011–2012

	Mechanical, electrical, and aerospace engineering		Aircraft mechanics and avionics	
	Recipients	Total Amount	Recipients	Total amount
Federal grants	90,581	$724 million	142,708	$918 million
Federal work study	30,583	$180 million	6,438	$47 million
Federal loans	120,740	$1.6 billion	114,564	$1.3 billion

Source: GAO analysis of Education data.

Notes: Federal loans do not include Plus Loans.

Education categorizes all degree programs through a CIP code which can be matched to a SOC code. This relationship indicates that educational programs classified in the CIP category prepare individuals directly for jobs classified in the SOC. For this data source, the National Postsecondary Student Aid Study (NPSAS), only 4 of the 6 digits of the CIP code are used. As a result, programs may be classified at a higher level and include related programs. With regard to aircraft mechanics and avionics, the CIP code used (47.06) includes programs related to vehicle maintenance and repair, such as automotive mechanics and engine mechanics. For electrical engineering, the CIP code used (14.10) includes programs related to telecommunications and optical engineering. The CIP codes used for mechanical (14.19) and aerospace (14.02) engineering did not have any additional programs associated with them.

DOL also provides grant moneys to various entities that support aviation-related training. For example, since 2011, through its Trade Adjustment Assistance Community College and Career Training Grant Program, DOL has provided more than $55 million to community colleges in California, Idaho, Kansas, Michigan, and Washington to support training in aviation manufacturing and machining, composites, and engineering technology. Through DOL's H-1B Technical Skills Training and Job Accelerator Innovation Challenge Grant Programs, DOL has provided more than $14.5 million to universities and localities to provide aerospace and aviation-related education, training, and job placement assistance directly related to high-growth occupations for which employers are currently using the H-1B nonimmigrant visa program to hire foreign workers and to support regional development.

Despite the availability of these programs, most employers and stakeholders we interviewed told us that maintaining a qualified aviation professional workforce will be more difficult in the future due to changes in K-12 education, a perceived emphasis on earning a 4-year degree, and the perceived decreased desirability for working in aviation, particularly aviation maintenance. Several employers cited the absence of vocational and "shop" classes in high school as a reason interest and critical knowledge in maintenance are waning. Several employers and stakeholders we interviewed also said that with parents and counselors insisting that a college degree is needed for every job, students may not be aware that there are well-paying professions that do not require a 4- year degree. FAA echoed this sentiment in describing the challenges of AVSED. According to AVSED, it can be difficult to interest students in aviation maintenance careers because it is mistakenly perceived to be a low paying, low skilled occupation. To combat this perception, according to stakeholders, AVSED and industry must find a means to convince parents and guidance counselors that not all well-paying careers require a bachelor's degree. Several employers and stakeholders also noted that aviation used to be a more "exciting" industry, which attracted people even though wages were often lower than other, similar industries. Events of the last decade—including September 2001 and airline bankruptcies and mergers—also have resulted in the aviation industry being viewed as unstable, compared to other industries.

Employers and stakeholders we spoke with did not agree about how to encourage entry into aviation occupations. Some suggested that FAA should do more to champion the industry and increase its outreach and educational efforts. Others suggested that by providing subsidies or tax credits, government could incentivize students to enter aviation fields and businesses to hire them. However, others maintained that government should not have a role and that it was an issue for industry to address. One company suggested that companies could sponsor students in exchange for an agreement that, upon graduation, they would work for a specified period of time for that company. Aerotek, a staffing solutions company that focuses on aviation, recently instituted a similar program when it collaborated with two aviation maintenance schools in Canada to train workers. According to Aerotek, it participated in the curriculum design to include topics its clients seek and guaranteed the classes would be full. Students who complete the program are then guaranteed employment. Aerotek estimated that it trained between 600 and 700 employees in this way.

AGENCY COMMENTS

We provided a draft of this report to the departments of Defense (DOD), Education (Education), Labor (DOL), and Transportation (DOT) for review and comment. We received technical comments on this report from Education, DOL, and DOT which were incorporated as appropriate. DOD did have any comments on the report.

Gerald L. Dillingham, Ph.D.
Director, Physical Infrastructure Issues

APPENDIX I: OBJECTIVE, SCOPE, AND METHODOLOGY

Our report focuses on the supply of and demand for individuals in three selected aviation professions–aerospace engineers, aircraft mechanics, and avionics technicians–which are involved in the design, manufacture, and repair of aircraft and have been the subject of concerns voiced by industry stakeholders. In this report, we examined: (1) what available data and forecasts reveal about the need for and potential availability of aerospace engineers, aircrafts mechanics, and avionics technicians and (2) what actions industry and the federal government are taking, if any, to help attract and retain these professionals.

To determine what available data reveal about the current need for and availability of these professionals, we reviewed relevant economic literature that describe labor market conditions,[1] developed a summary of the general economic principles for evaluating labor market conditions, and identified relevant data sources. Economic literature states that no single measure exists to determine whether a labor shortage exists; however, one can look at multiple indicators— including unemployment rates, employment numbers, and earnings—that might converge to suggest either the presence or absence of a shortage.[2] We obtained these data from the Bureau of Labor Statistics (BLS) Current Population Survey for years 2000 through 2012.[3] In 2010 BLS adopted the updated Standard Occupational Classifications (SOC) titles and, as a result, some occupation's names changed during the time period we examined. We used SAS, a statistical software application, to connect data for 2000– 2010 and 2011–2012 by the SOC titles and did not include occupations for which no exact job title match existed between the two time periods; this did not affect our occupations of interest.[4] We analyzed how these indicators have changed over time, and whether these indicators suggest a labor shortage–that is, whether there appears to be an imbalance between the labor supply (i.e., available people) and demand (i.e., available jobs). We analyzed each occupation relative to all other occupations and using an absolute scale with benchmarks developed in previous economic analysis.[5] For the unemployment rate we looked at the average unemployment rate for each occupation from 2000 through 2012.[6] For both employment and earnings we analyzed any change from 2000 through 2012.[7] To verify our results, we discussed them with Malcolm Cohen, PhD, labor economist and author of the original indicator analysis.[8] We incorporated his comments as appropriate. Finally, we summarized limitations with the data with respect to how we used them. To assess the reliability of BLS's CPS data we reviewed documentation related to the data sources from prior GAO reports and BLS's technical documentation about the quality of the data. We determined the data were sufficiently reliable for the purposes of our indicator analysis to provide context on the labor market.

To identify future demand for, supply of, or employment projections for individuals in our selected aviation professions, we performed a literature review of scholarly material, government reports, and books, among others; identified any projections for aviation professional occupations; and analyzed results that projected demand in the United States (or North America) using databases that included ProQuest, WorldCat, and LexisNexis. We identified three studies—one performed by the federal government (BLS) and two performed by industry (the Boeing Company and the International Civil Aviation Organization (ICAO))–and obtained the most recent analysis for each.[9] To understand these projections, we reviewed the processes, methodologies, and sources of information used to make the projections. We also discussed the projections with the staff that performed each study. We did not verify the data that the companies collected and used in making their projections. We also described, based on economic literature, why forecasting these factors generally includes a great deal of uncertainty.

To identify trends in sources of supply for individuals in our selected aviation professions we obtained data through 2012 from sources that supply such professionals. We analyzed the Department of Education's (Education) data on annual completions by major since academic year 2000–2001; data from the Department of Defense (DOD) on service members separating from the military since fiscal year 2000; and the Federal Aviation Administration's (FAA) data on the number of people annually obtaining airframe and power plant (A&P) certificates since 2000.[10] Specifically:

- *Education:* To describe national trends in number of completions in aviation-related majors we analyzed data from Education's Integrated Postsecondary Education Data System (IPEDS). We used Education's Classification of Instructional Programs (CIP) and matched degree codes to our SOC codes to identify the relevant degree programs. Specifically, the CIP-SOC relationship indicates that programs classified in the CIP category prepare individuals directly for jobs classified in the SOC category. Our analysis of IPEDS data included all schools that reported enrollment data in these fields.
- *DOD:* To better understand the role of the U.S. military as a source for our selected professions, we obtained data on service members separating from the armed forces (i.e., the Navy, Army, Air Force, and Marine Corps); the current number of aviation maintenance workers in the military; and forecasted rates of separation for maintenance workers.[11] We also interviewed military officials at the Pentagon to understand how separation trends in the future might compare to past trends. Data for aircraft mechanics includes avionics technicians. DOD was unable to provide data on aerospace engineers.
- *FAA:* To better understand trends in the number of new A&P certificates issued and age distribution of current certificate-holders, we obtained data from FAA on A&P certificates issued from 2000 through 2012, by the type of training the certificate-holder received.

We also obtained data from FAA on A&P certificate-holders as of July 2013 and, using STATA, developed descriptive statistics, including the distribution of certificates held by age and the total number of certificates held by those age 70 or younger. The database in which certificate-holder information is stored maintains records on individuals until FAA is informed of their death. To better estimate the number of active A&P mechanics, we excluded individuals over the age of 70.

To assess the reliability of Education, DOD, and FAA data we reviewed documentation related to these data sources from our prior reports, and agencies' websites, and interviewed knowledgeable government officials about the quality of the data. After analysis, we determined that the data were sufficiently reliable to provide general trends in the sources of supply of individuals in the selected aviation professions.[12] We supplemented data with interviews from government, industry, 7 select aviation engineering, maintenance, and avionics training programs, and unions representing aviation professionals. Schools were selected to provide a range of perspectives in location, size, and type of program. Where possible we selected schools in cities where we interviewed employers. Information collected from these interviews is not generalizable.

To supplement these broader trends, we selected 23 employers from FAA's list of certificated repair stations and air carriers—including original equipment manufacturers (manufacturers), air carriers, and maintenance, repair, and overhaul facilities (repair stations)—across the United States to understand the extent to which specific employers experienced difficulty attracting and retaining workers and any actions that have been taken. (For a complete list of employers, see table 6.) We selected companies based on consideration of several factors, including the total number of mechanics and repairpersons employed, the ratio of A&P– certificated mechanics to non-certificated mechanics, type of work performed, and geographic location. We limited our scope to employers located within the United States. To develop our list of actions that employers may take to mitigate labor shortages, we reviewed economic literature and interviewed the authors.[13] Using semi-structured interviews, we asked all employers whether they had used each action mentioned in economic literature to attract and retain personnel and, if they had taken that action, the purpose for doing so.[14] We also asked employers about the extent to which they expect hiring and retention to improve or become more difficult in the future.

Table 6. Selected Employers, Location, Type of Interview, and Type of Employer

Employer	Location selected	Type of employer	Method of interview
AAR Aircraft Services, Incorporated	Indianapolis, IN	Repair station	Phone
Aviation and Defense, Inc.	San Bernardino, CA	Repair station	In person
Capital Aviation Instrument Corporation	Manassas, VA	Repair station	In person
Century Flight Systems, Inc.	Mineral Wells, TX	Repair station	In person
Certified Aviation Services	Ontario, CA	Repair station	In person
Delta Airlines	Atlanta, GA	Repair station and airline	In person
Epps Air Service	Atlanta, GA	Repair station	In person
Excel Aviation	Gainesville, TX	Repair station	In person
FedEx Express	Los Angeles, CA and Memphis, TN	Repair station and airline	Phone
Gulfstream Aerospace Corporation	Long Beach, CA	Repair station and manufacturer	In person
Hawker Beechcraft	Atlanta, GA	Repair station and manufacturer	In person
Jet Works Air Center Management, LLC	Denton, TX	Repair station	In person
King Aerospace	Ardmore, OK	Repair station	In person
Lockheed Martin Aircraft Center	Greenville, SC	Manufacturer	Phone
Piedmont Airlines, Inc.	Salisbury, MD	Airline	In person
Precision Electronics	Atlanta, GA	Repair station	In person
Rockwell Collins Inc.	Atlanta, GA	Repair station	In person
Signature Flight Support	Dulles, VA	Repair station	In person
Southwest Airlines	Dallas, TX	Airline	In person
Texas Pneumatic Systems, Inc.	Arlington, TX	Repair station	In person
TIMCO Aviation Services	Greensboro, NC	Repair Station	In person
The Boeing Company	Renton, WA	Manufacturer	Phone
West Coast Aircraft Maintenance	Long Beach, CA	Repair station	In person

Source: GAO analysis of FAA data.

Note: Many of the companies we interviewed have repair stations in multiple locations. When possible, we sought to gather information about each of their locations or differences between locations during our interviews.

We then performed a content analysis of our interviews to summarize the extent to which these actions were taken across companies. We completed 19 of the 23 interviews in person during site visits to 7 states—California, Georgia, Maryland, North Carolina, Oklahoma, Texas, and Virginia. The findings from our interviews with selected employers should not be used to make generalizations about the views of all employers; however, employers' observations related to their ability to fill job vacancies are a component of analyses that seek to corroborate the existence of an occupational labor shortage. As such, the information gathered in these interviews sought to supplement analyses of national-level labor market data with employer experiences.

To understand the federal government's role, including funding provided for aviation-related training, and any actions government has taken to support the aviation industry and our selected aviation professions, we identified the relevant federal agencies through interviews with stakeholders, analysis of our prior reports, and a literature review. The identified agencies were: FAA, DOD, Veterans Affairs, and DOL. We interviewed officials to understand the programs each agency operates that either target the specific occupations or could be used to support the occupations. We also examined relevant programs, laws, and regulations. For DOD's aircraft–maintenance certification program and for DOL's Workforce Investment Act-supported training, the respective agencies provided us with the number of individuals that participated in or completed the program. To describe federal student aid awarded to students enrolled in aviation-related majors we analyzed data from Education's National Postsecondary Student Aid Study (NPSAS) 2011-2012—a survey of a nationally representative sample of students. NPSAS is a comprehensive study that examines how students and their families pay for higher education; data are based on administrative records and student interviews and include students who received financial aid and those who did not. Similar to our analysis of IPEDS data, we used Education's CIP categories and matched degree programs to our SOC codes of interest to identify the relevant degree programs. Unless noted, all estimates from NPSAS are within 5 percentage points.

We conducted this performance audit from February 2013 through February 2014 in accordance with generally accepted government auditing standards. Those standards require that we plan and perform the audit to obtain sufficient, appropriate evidence to provide a reasonable basis for our findings and conclusions based on our audit objectives. We believe that the evidence obtained provides a reasonable basis for our findings and conclusions based on our audit objectives.

End Notes

[1] GAO recently conducted similar work looking at the supply and demand of commercial airline pilots. See GAO, *Commercial Aviation: Information on the Supply and Demand of Airline Pilots*, GAO-14-232 (Washington, D.C: Feb. 28, 2014).

[2] See, for example, Malcolm Cohen, *Labor Shortages as America Approaches the Twenty-first Century* (Ann Arbor, MI: University of Michigan Press, July 1, 1995).

[3] DOD could not provide data on the number of service members separating from all branches of the military for fiscal year 2000. To allow for comparisons across all years, we only reported data since fiscal year 2001.

[4] In addition to aerospace engineers, mechanical and electrical engineers, among others, are employed by the aviation industry.

[5] Military applicants may have supplemented work experience with training through the Joint Services Aviation Maintenance Technician Certification (JSAMTCC) program. Military applicants who have not completed the JSAMTCC program must be able to demonstrate experience in 50 percent of curriculum subject areas for the ratings sought. The JSAMTCC program is discussed in additional detail later in this report.

[6] In addition to education and training requirements, individuals must be at least 18 years of age and be able to read, write, speak, and understand English to be eligible for certification.

[7] Repair-person certificates may be issued for a variety of tasks including, among others, welding and painting.

[8] Unlike an A&P certificate that is issued to an individual, a repair-person certificate is issued to a person through an FAA-approved repair station and, as a result, is only valid while that person is performing the specific task at the issuing station.

[9] There are no current or historical data available on the number of enrollees and graduates of those schools, and FAA does not require the schools to report this information.

[10] FAA does not approve air carrier's maintenance programs; it issues carrier operations specifications that authorize the carrier to use a maintenance program and the air-carrier maintenance manual required by FAA regulations. Advisory Circular 120-16F.

[11] We were unable to analyze information on avionics technicians because the sample size for the data was too small.

[12] As mentioned, a labor shortage occurs when demand for workers for a particular occupation is greater than the number ("supply") of workers who are qualified, available, and willing to do the work at a certain wage rate.

[13] All data presented in this review on the unemployment rate, employment, and earnings are from BLS's CPS data unless otherwise noted. Data from BLS on earnings have been adjusted for inflation.

[14] Cohen, *Labor Shortages*.

[15] Cohen, *Labor Shortages*. This assumes that unemployed individuals will likely seek work in the same occupation in which they were previously employed.

[16] Cohen, *Labor Shortages*. Cohen developed an absolute scale with seven categories to more easily synthesize results from the indicators. Each indicator is assigned a numerical value from 1 to 7 based on benchmarks that were derived by examining distributions of results

and identifying natural groupings (e.g., distinguishing between positive and negative employment growth). A rating of "7" means than an indicator is most consistent with a labor shortage and a "1" means that the indicator is most consistent with a labor surplus.

[17] For the economy overall, since 2000, the average unemployment rate has been 6.3 percent, earnings and employment has stayed about the same, according to BLS.

[18] For this time period unemployment rates ranged from 0.6 percent to 22.2 percent across the different occupations.

[19] Cohen, *Labor Shortages*. Growth rates for the change in employment, and earnings were calculated by fitting a time trend using a log linear regression, for which we computed statistical significance. As such, our calculations yield different larger annual changes compared to calculating the percentage change over the same time period and annualizing the percentage change because our method does not include the effect of compounding. While results show larger changes than an annualized analysis would, both values were within the range to receive a 5. Further, calculating the data this way allowed us to calculate the significance of any trends.

[20] In Cohen's book, the indicator levels for earning growth are presented in nominal terms, without accounting for inflation. They were developed using years 1983-1993. In order to use them for the period 2000 through 2012, when inflation has been lower, we adjusted them using the average inflation rates for the earlier period. Based on the adjusted scale, both occupations would receive a 4 (out of seven), although the real rate of growth in wages is close to zero.

[21] From 2000 through 2012 aircraft mechanics had the 70th lowest unemployment rate (out of 295 occupations).

[22] The growth rate for aircraft mechanics was negative and was the 265th highest out of 490 occupations.

[23] BLS collects a Job Openings and Labor Turnover Survey that provides a broad measure of job vacancies, but not by occupation.

[24] Carolyn Veneri, "Can Occupational Labor Shortages be Identified Using Available Data," *Monthly Labor Review* (March 1999) 15-21.

[25] Data are not available for avionics technicians because the workforce is too small and BLS did not publicly report data for all years. Further, these data for aerospace engineers and aircraft mechanics are from the CPS survey and represent the number of people, both employed and unemployed that either are or were most recently employed in these occupations. BLS uses the term aircraft mechanics and service technicians to describe individuals that repair, maintain, and service aircraft.

[26] Education categorizes all degree programs through a Classification of Instructional Programs (CIP); each CIP code is then matched to the SOC. This relationship indicates that programs classified in the CIP category prepare individuals directly for jobs classified in the SOC category. For our analysis of Education data, we included CIP programs that prepare individuals directly to our occupations of interest. For aerospace engineers, this included the following degree programs: aerospace, aeronautical and astronautical/space engineering engineering (CIP code 14.0201), mechanical engineering (CIP code 14.1901), and electrical and electronics engineering (CIP code 14.1001).

[27] The related CIP codes for aircraft mechanic included airframe mechanics and aircraft maintenance technology (CIP code 47.0607), aircraft power-plant technology (CIP code 47.0608), and agricultural mechanics and equipment technology (CIP code 01.0205), whereas avionics technicians only included avionics maintenance technology/technician (CIP code 47.0609).

[28] FAA does not require approved AMT schools to provide data on enrollments or graduation rates.

[29] DOD data for aircraft mechanics include avionics technicians. DOD was unable to provide data for engineers.

[30] We also reviewed two industry studies that projected maintenance employment within the aviation industry worldwide and by region–one published by The International Civil Aviation Organization (ICAO) and one by the Boeing Company (Boeing). The ICAO study forecasted future employment demand and the available supply of maintenance personnel based on existing training capacity, but did not produce a projected rate of growth. The Boeing study projected employment for personnel employed to maintain commercial aircraft and found that to meet future anticipated demand, including the effects of anticipated retirements and attrition, approximately 97,900 new aviation maintenance workers will be need to be hired in North America by 2032. We were unable to assess the reliability of these studies due to a lack of sufficient information about their methods and assumptions. For more information on these forecasts see the International Civil Aviation Organization, *Global and Regional 20-year Forecasts: Pilots, Maintenance Personnel, and Air Traffic Controllers* (2011) and the *Boeing Company Current Market Outlook, 2013-2032.*

[31] This would result in an annualized growth rate of about 0.71 percent per year. Employment growth in this area is relatively low because aerospace engineers are typically employed in manufacturing industries that are projected to grow slowly or decline. Demand for aerospace engineers will be greatest in areas related to national defense and the design of civilian aircraft, according to BLS.

[32] Employment for aircraft mechanics and service technicians is projected to be 124,700 in 2022 (an annualized growth rate of about 0.24), and employment of avionics technicians is projected to be 17,600 in 2022 (an annualized growth rate of about 0.29).

[33] Specifically, during the 2012 to 2022 timeframe, BLS estimates there will be 25,400 job openings for aerospace engineers, 35,600 job openings for aircraft mechanics and service technicians, and 4,000 job openings for avionics technicians.

[34] GAO, *Aviation Safety: FAA Needs to Update Curriculum and Certification Requirements for Aviation Mechanics,* GAO-03-317 (Washington, D.C.: Mar 6, 2003).

[35] Partly in response to previous GAO work (GAO-03-317), FAA convened an Aviation Rulemaking Advisory Committee (ARAC). In 2007, FAA assigned the ARAC a new task: to review and recommend revisions to certain requirements for operation of AMT schools. In 2009, the ARAC submitted recommendations to FAA that included: (1) creating a curriculum review board to biennially review and recommend changes and (2) changing the distribution of training hours between subjects to 450 hours for general knowledge, 800 hours for airframe, and 650 hours for power plant. According to FAA, it implemented the recommendation to create the review board, chaired by the Aviation Technical Education Council, which began operation in fiscal year 2014.

[36] Burt S. Barnow, John Trutko, and Jaclyn Piatak, "Conceptual Basis for Identifying and Measuring Occupational Labor Shortages." In *Occupational Labor Shortages: Concepts, Causes, Consequences, and Cures* (Kalamazoo, MI: W.E. Upjohn Institute for Employment Research, 2013) 1-34.

[37] On May 11, 1996, a ValuJet DC-9 crashed into the Florida Everglades shortly after takeoff from Miami International Airport, killing all 110 people aboard. Earlier that year, FAA had initiated a special review of the rapidly growing low, cost carrier following a series of incidents and non-fatal accidents. In June 1996, FAA announced that the carrier would

cease operations pending safety improvements to address serious deficiencies it had found in ValuJet's airworthiness, maintenance, quality oversight, and engineering capabilities. This sparked renewed criticism of the Department of Transportation and FAA because it appeared to contrast with statements, made following the accident, assuring the public that the airline was safe. The next day, the Secretary of Transportation committed to urge Congress to make safety FAA's single primary mission. The change was codified in the Federal Aviation Reauthorization Act of 1996, Pub.L. No. 104-264, § 401, 110 Stat. 3213, 3255.

[38] GAO, *Managing for Results: Critical Actions for Measuring Performance*, T-GGD/AIMD95-187 (Washington, D.C.: June 20, 1995).

[39] Section 558 of the National Defense Authorization Act (NDAA) for Fiscal Year 2012, Pub. L. No. 112-81, 125 Stat. 1298, 1418 (2011), as amended by section 543 of NDAA for Fiscal Year 2013, Pub. L. No. 112-239, 126 Stat. 1632, 1737, required DOD to carry out a pilot program to assess the feasibility and advisability of permitting enlisted members of the Armed Forces to obtain civilian credentialing or licensing for skills required for military occupational specialties or qualification for duty specialty codes. In addition to aircraft mechanics, the pilot included automotive mechanics, healthcare support, logistics and supply, and truck drivers.

[40] As previously noted, military aircraft mechanics are not required to hold an A&P certification and may not understand the additional autonomy tasks—such as returning a plane to service—and career opportunities available to civilian mechanics who hold a certificate as compared to those who do not.

[41] National Defense Authorization Act, Fiscal Year 1991, Pub. L. No. 101-510, § 502(a)(1), 104 Stat. 1485, 1553 (1990).

[42] In 2011, the Administration redesigned TAP—the first major re-design of the program since its inception over 20 years ago. As part of the redesign, all service members are required to meet career readiness standards—the completion of a set of tasks that demonstrate their readiness for a civilian career. In response to a congressional mandate, GAO is in the process of assessing DOD's implementation of the program redesign. Pub. L. No. 112-56, § 226, 125 Stat. 711, 719 (2011).

[43] Amount is for academic year 2013-2014 for individuals who are eligible for the full benefit level.

[44] GAO, *VA Education Benefits: VA Needs to Improve Program Management and Provide More Timely Information to Students,* GAO-13-338 (Washington, D.C.: May 22, 2013).

[45] Pub. L. No. 105-220, 112 Stat. 936 (1998).

[46] As part of the eligibility conditions for WIA-supported training services, individuals must be unable to obtain grant assistance from other sources to pay the costs of such training, including Welfare-to-Work, state-funded training funds, Trade Adjustment Assistance, and Federal Pell Grants established under title IV of the Higher Education Act of 1965, or require WIA assistance in addition to other sources of grant assistance, including Federal Pell Grants. 20 C.F.R. § 663.310(d). DOL does not collect information on the total amount of WIA resources expended on training.

[47] From 2010 through 2012, 269 individuals received funding for avionics technician training, 1,527 for aircraft mechanics and service technician training, 134 for aerospace engineering training, and 296 for aerospace engineering and operations technician training. During that time, a total of 691,343 individuals with associated information on occupation of training received training supported, in whole or part, by WIA funds.

End Notes for Appendix I

[1] See Burt S. Barnow, John Trutko, and Jaclyn Piatak, "*Conceptual Basis for Identifying and Measuring Occupational Labor Shortages,*" in Occupational *Labor Shortages: Concepts, Causes, Consequences, and Cures.* (Kalamazoo, MI: W.E. Upjohn Institute for Employment Research, 2013) 1-3;4 and Malcolm S. Cohen *Labor Shortages: As America Approaches the Twenty-First Century* (Ann Arbor, MI: University of Michigan Press, 1995).

[2] In the absence of a universally agreed upon definition we have defined a labor shortage in the same terms that have been used in economic literature, including a Bureau of Labor statistics (BLS) publication.

[3] The Current Population Survey, a monthly household survey conducted by the Bureau of the Census for the BLS, provides a comprehensive body of information on the employment and unemployment experience of the nation's population, classified by age, sex, race, and a variety of other characteristics.

[4] BLS adopted the modified SOC titles in 2010 and as a result, some occupations were combined and others were phased out. While this did not affect our occupations, it affected the total number of occupations. We excluded those occupations for which the name changed. We also excluded occupations that had any years where the sample size was too small (i.e., under 50,000 observations) to report unemployment, median weekly earnings, or employment. This resulted in 288, 490, and 250 occupations in unemployment rate, employment, and earnings, respectively.

[5] Cohen developed a scale with seven categories to more easily synthesize results from the indictors. Each occupation's indicators were assigned a numerical value from 1 to 7. Categories were developed by looking at the distribution of the results and setting natural groupings (e.g. distinguishing between positive and negative employment growth). A rank of "7" designates the indicator is consistent with a labor shortage and a "1" designates the indicator is consistent with a labor surplus.

[6] As part of a sensitivity analysis we also compared data since 2003, in addition to developing a regression line for both time periods. Performing multiple analyses with different comparison years allowed us to ensure that a year with unique results would not impact our analysis.

[7] Similar to the unemployment rate we also looked at data since 2003 as well. Finally, we adjusted earnings for inflation and only included full-time non-farm workers.

[8] Malcolm S. Cohen, President of Employment Research Corporation, received his PhD in economics from the Massachusetts Institute of Technology in 1967. He has directed numerous labor market research and forecasting studies for the U.S. Department of Labor. He testifies as an expert witness in various court proceedings on economic loss, discrimination and other employment issues.

[9] For BLS we summarized employment projections from 2012 through 2022. The ICAO study forecasted future employment demand and the available supply of maintenance personnel based on existing training capacity, but did not produce a projected rate of growth. The Boeing study projected employment for personnel employed to maintain commercial aircraft. We were unable to assess the reliability of these studies due to a lack of sufficient information about their methods and assumptions. For more information on these forecasts see the International Civil Aviation Organization, Global and Regional 20- year Forecasts: Pilots, Maintenance Personnel, and Air Traffic Controllers (2011) and the Boeing Company Current Market Outlook, 2013–2032 (Boeing, 2013).

[10] DOD could not provide data on the number of service members separating from all branches of the military before fiscal year 2000. To allow for comparisons across all years, we only reported data since fiscal year 2001.

[11] Data from DOD are current as of June 17, 2013.

[12] Due to concerns regarding how DOD calculates its rate of workers leaving the military and how rates varied across each branch we did not report this information. Rather we reported the number of people instead.

[13] Barnow, Trutko, and Piatak, "Identifying and Measuring Occupational Labor Shortages."

[14] Barnow, Trutko, and Piatak, "Identifying and Measuring Occupational Labor Shortages." These actions include increasing recruiting efforts, increasing the use of overtime, reducing the minimum qualifications for the job, restructuring the work to use current or new employees in other occupations, substituting machinery and equipment for labor, training workers for jobs, improving working conditions, offering bonuses to new employees, improving wages and fringe benefits, contracting out the work, and turning down work.

INDEX